Hiking the San Juan Islands

Island Hikes & Walks
in San Juan, Skagit & Island Counties

Ken Wilcox

Plus Parks, Viewpoints, Water Access & Campgrounds

Northwest Wild Books
Bellingham, Washington

Hiking the San Juan Islands
Island Hikes & Walks in San Juan, Skagit & Island Counties

© 2001 by Ken Wilcox

ISBN 0-9617879-5-3

Photography by Steve Satushek (four cover images) and the author (all others). Maps by Steve Walker (Middle Fork GIS) and the author. Designed and published by Northwest Wild Books, Bellingham, WA. No old-growth trees were harmed by the printing of this book. Manufactured in the USA.

Front cover. top: Ewing Cove (Wilcox); bottom left to right: Deception Pass Bridge (Satushek), Mount Constitution (Satushek),white fawn lilies (Wilcox)
Back cover. clockwise: South Whidbey State Park (Wilcox), Lime Kiln Point (Satushek), intertidal life (Wilcox), chairs (Satushek)

Books by Northwest Wild Books...
Hiking Whatcom County, 3rd Edition (1996, 2000)
Hiking Snohomish County (1998)
Hiking the San Juan Islands (2001)

Coming soon...
Hiking Skagit County

We welcome your comments, corrections, kudos, criticisms, and suggestions regarding current and future editions of these titles. Write us at Northwest Wild Books, P. O. Box 4003, Bellingham, WA 98227.

DISCLAIMER

This guidebook is intended for use by competent hikers who accept the inherent and sometimes unpredictable hazards associated with outdoor activity. Read the introductory material and be sure of your ability to safely hike any of the trails listed before venturing out. This book is NOT a boaters guide. Always travel these waters with an experienced boater familiar with local conditions, navigation, marine communications, emergency procedures, and the ever-present risks of changing weather, tides, currents, rocks, poor visibility, other marine traffic, and the like. Navigating the islands can be treacherous for the inexperienced and ill-prepared.
The user assumes all risks!

Contents

{} = EASIER HIKES   **{} {} {} =** MORE DIFFICULT HIKES

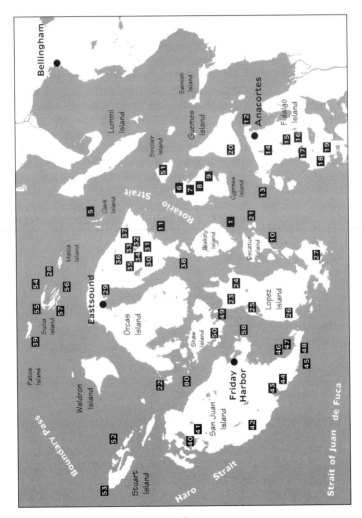

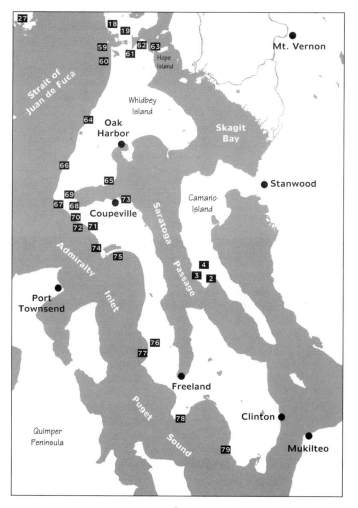

Rosario Head, Fidalgo Island

For my friends, Tom Kirtz and Dave Wenzler,
somewhere out there on the trail...

FOREWORD

I remember the first time I boarded the ferry at Anacortes for the short cruise to the San Juans, island gems of Washington's unnamed inland sea. It was in the 1970s, before my hopeless addiction to hiking had fully materialized. We leaned against the white rail, a cold sea breeze licking our faces, and wondered why we hadn't made the trip years before. I recall images of the ferry dock slipping behind us, Guemes Channel and Fidalgo Head receding quietly against the green-gray horizon, and new lands sliding into view: Cypress, Decatur, Blakely, Lopez. We disembarked, visited Spencer Spit, and walked the beach where invisible goeducks squirted alarm at our soggy footsteps.

Few other memories remain from that trip, but I know I came away satisfied that I had finally been to the islands. In the islands is a feeling of place that goes beyond the obvious. Many are drawn to the abundance of scenic coastline, quiet living, and relative isolation from the I-5 car-culture on the mainland and its cancerous outgrowth of suburban sprawl. In fact, when you spend a little time traveling through the islands, you really begin to notice how much automobiles are adversely impacting our lives and the environment. The correlation between cars and quality of place becomes clear. Islands that are linked to the mainland by bridges (and thus, the most easily accessed by car) have become highly suburbanized and much less isolated, while even the islands served by car ferries are suffering similar effects, but to a much lesser degree (see Hike 47 for news of a frightening proposal for a new county road on San Juan Island that could destroy a major corridor through American Camp).. Some islands without regular ferry service still have roads and cars, yet more difficult access has helped preserve the qualities that have attracted people to the island life there for generations.

None of this is surprising, but the observations may help us understand why Northwest living just isn't what it used to be. In the islands, the correlation between quality of life and the density of automobiles seems clear and direct. On the mainland, it's a more confused picture, but surely just as real. As roads become crowded, we build more roads, add more lanes. But rather than relieving congestion, as traffic engineers are grudgingly beginning to acknowledge, we are simply inviting people to drive more. Thus we are spreading the same traffic congestion over larger areas, impacting more people, more communities, more streams and wetlands, and more wildlife habitat, while depleting resources and speeding up climate change. Counter-intuitive as it may seem, we would probably be far better off with *fewer* roads—and instead, focus more of our hard-earned tax dollars on facilities for walking, biking, boating, and public transit.

Speaking of which... most of the islands listed in this guide can be easily accessed on foot or by bicycle, while public transit service is also available for many areas. Nevertheless, a car does come in handy in some places, especially Orcas Island, where the long and winding road to Moran State Park makes the trails there more of a challenge to reach by bike. Detailed information is provided in this guide for various transportation options to consider when making plans to visit the islands.

Many of the more remote islands can only be reached by small boat, whether you hire one out or row your own. Experienced mariners are at a distinct advantage in exploring the quiet treasures of the less traveled islands. If you aren't one of them, there's still hope. Foot-ferries and water taxis serve some of these out-of-the-way places. Commercial guides and kayaking tours are other options or learn to kayak yourself, but learn from someone who knows. *Wind and currents around the islands pose very real threats to the ill-prepared.* Of course, it always helps to have a friend with a nice boat (maybe help paint the hull or cook the meals in exchange for cruising).

The geographical scope of this guide encompasses not only the San Juans, but the surrounding archipelago of more than 200 named islands in San Juan, Skagit, and Island Counties. Only a few dozen islands, however, are accessible to the public, fewer have trails or beaches to walk, and only seven are easily reached by car. These include the four ferried islands (Lopez, Shaw, Orcas, and San Juan), and three islands reached by bridge (Whidbey, Camano, and Fidalgo).

At least half the islands in the archipelago are really just rocks that aren't normally submerged at higher tides, or rocky islets that don't even support a tree. However, many of these do support marine birds and mammals, and 84 of them are within the San Juan Islands National Wildlife Refuge (82 of which are officially off limits in order to protect sensitive, threatened, or endangered species). Many other small islands are privately owned, but offer no public facilities or access, other than an occasional public beach or rocky tideland. Some of these smaller private islands are also managed for wildlife, and some are developed. In addition to the refuge islands, a number of others are either publicly owned or include significant areas that are managed as marine state parks or recreation sites, generally accessible to small boats.

Hiking the San Juan Islands covers hikes and beach walks for nearly two dozen islands. The guide also includes information on islands which lack opportunities for major rambling but are still interesting to visit, as well as some islands that are private or off limits, to help visitors avoid intruding into areas where they don't belong.

The larger islands, most notably Orcas, San Juan, Fidalgo, and Whidbey, account for the bulk of the hikes, as well as the hiking miles, in this guide. Whidbey is one of the largest islands in the lower forty-eight states, and it is the most populated of all the islands listed. Despite the multitude of cars zipping up and down the center of island, Whidbey offers an extraordinary selection of state and local parks and unique natural landscapes, and many miles of public beaches and maintained trails from which to choose.

From a 5-mile hike on the beach below dramatic 300-foot high bluffs, to a steep trudge up Mount Constitution or a short stroll to the storm-swept coast at Shark Reef, the islands of northwest Washington are truly superb, and offer plenty of hiking for people of all ages and abilities. Hopefully, this guide will be most helpful to those who, like me, are just beginning to discover the place.

Happy trails,

Ken Wilcox, June, 2001

Acknowledgments

First of all, an enthusiastic island wave to Glen and Mary for putting me up on Lopez, and to Glen especially for many enjoyable miles on the water and on the trail, solving most of the world's problems along the way. Huge thanks to Vic and his mother ship, the Galaxy, and the incredible salmon, the onboard "hot tub," the remote office, and the flexibility to help get me where I needed to go. To Keith and Kiko I am particularly grateful not only for the good company on the trail and in the boats, but for offering suggestions and observations.

Appreciation also goes to Steve Satushek for his photographic contributions to this book, as well as two previous guides to the mainland; to Erin Moore for her impeccable editing services (any remaining errors are my own), Steve Walker at Middle Fork GIS who, like Erin, agreed to dive into the project on short notice; and to the handful of friends who helped me figure out what to put on the cover. The usual group hug goes to the friendly staff at Village Books in Bellingham and to Chuck and Dee for being so supportive of the work of local writers. Appreciation goes to Fiona Cohen at the Bellingham Herald for taking an interest in the project and for joining me for a day of "field research."

In the islands, I also appreciate the hospitality that people seem to offer wherever you go, like that of the Mills on Stuart Island where we tied up the Galaxy and heard great fish stories... and the mail guru (was it Ferdi?), making his weekly run to Sinclair Island... and Phil, the caretaker at The Nature Conservancy's Yellow Island Preserve, quick to offer clear details on the island's history and ecology... and Richard Osborne, the whale guy (they seem to follow him everywhere)... and Bob Myhr of the San Juan Preservation Trust for important insights and friendly suggestions.

Thanks also to the helpful county planning and library staff at Friday Harbor; to Lee McFarland, Don Mason, and Jill Wood with Island County for the latest on trails there; to Billy, Gary, and Wilma for information on the marine state park system; and to other park staff and managers at many local and state parks who helped fill in the missing details; and to Kathy and other Department of Natural Resources staff for information on Cypress Island and other DNR sites.

A big thank you also to the many good friends who allowed me to drag them along to the islands, only to then hold them all back while I busily scribbled notes and snapped photographs: so thanks Harry, Kathy, Beth, and Pepper. Thanks also to my housemate, Ellen, for tolerating my total takeover of the kitchen; and finally, to Marc Bardsley and Wendy Steffensen for their enthusiastic support.

The Islands of San Juan, Skagit & Island Counties

INTRODUCTION

The famed San Juan Islands of northwest Washington State have long been known as a mecca for summer boating, while landlubber tourists have been crowding onto ferries for decades to experience some small part of the islands' cultural and geographical charm. The intimate experience of land and sea, and a preponderance of friendly islanders, offer travelers good odds for memorable adventures, large and small.

The geographical scope of this guide encompasses not only the San Juans, but the surrounding archipelago of more than 200 named islands in San Juan, Skagit, and Island Counties (another 200-plus rocks and reefs are unnamed). Only a few dozen islands, however, are accessible to the public, fewer have trails or beaches to walk, and only seven are easily reached by car. These include the four ferried islands (Lopez, Shaw, Orcas, and San Juan), and three islands reached by bridge (Whidbey, Camano, and Fidalgo). While San Juan County reaches to the middle of Rosario Strait, several of Skagit County's islands (Cypress, Guemes, and Sinclair) are not far beyond and are generally considered to fall within the San Juan group. Depending on whose geography you trust, Whatcom County's Lummi Island could be considered part of the group as well. Of all the islands listed, about 30 support year-round residents.

At least half the named islands in the archipelago are really just rocks that aren't normally submerged at higher tides, or rocky islets that don't even support a tree. However, many of these do support marine birds and mammals, and 84 of them are within the San Juan Islands National Wildlife Refuge; 82 of these are officially off limits in order to protect sensitive, threatened, or endangered species. Many other small islands (generally with trees) are privately owned, but offer no public facilities or access, other than an occasional public beach or rocky tideland. Some of these smaller private islands are also managed for wildlife, and some are developed. Additionally, a number of smaller islands, plus a few larger ones, are either publicly owned or include significant areas that are managed as marine state parks or recreation sites. These are often accessible by kayak, sailboat, or other small watercraft.

While boats and cars drive most of the exploring, other modern-day technological devices well suited to islanding are, of course, ...feet. Actually they are ancient tools, largely forgotten by certain sects, but still widely used in the art of "walking" in some societies. A lot of it at once is often called "hiking." Many of us who successfully apply this technology in our daily quest for adventure and cosmic enlightenment have enjoyed marked success—at least with the former. And surely you can too. So, by all means, get out of the car and take a hike. It's good for the environment, good for the mind-body thing, and might even result in something memorable.

In the San Juans, as well as the nearby islands of Skagit and Island Counties, trails and walkable beaches offer outstanding opportunities to immerse oneself in Northwest living. Trails wind through unique natural areas, historic sites—some of them pivotal in the development of Washington State—prehistoric sites, some of which were occupied by Native Americans for thousands of years, and a host of just plain beauteous places.

This guide describes 80 hikes on 22 different islands, ranging from an easy half-mile stroll to a much more strenuous trek up and over Orcas Island's Mount Constitution. The diversity of listings are intended to provide good geographic coverage for the region, as well as a wide array of hiking environments—from old-growth forests and lonely beaches to hidden lakes and scenic ridge-top meadows—while offering a range of difficulty levels to choose from.

In the islands, much awaits the willing adventurer. In fact, as more of us learn, like the "true" islanders, to let go of our clocks and schedules and forget about some of the hasty goals we set for ourselves in a workaday world, each of us could probably hit the trail more often—not that we all ought go to the same place at once! Yet with so many of us focused on the addictions of consumption and accumulating wealth (whether we're successful at it or not), we often forget about the paramount rewards that come from the simplest pleasures—like walking, or watching a tireless kingfisher buzzing the shore at dusk. A good hike inspires good thoughts about the real world (although I wonder sometimes which world that is).

Island Trails Overview

Island trails today...

Whether you're just starting out or have been hiking for decades, the islands of San Juan, Skagit, and Island Counties offer much fertile ground to explore. More than 200 miles of trails and perhaps 50 miles or more of walkable beaches are found on less than two dozen islands, though no comprehensive survey has ever been completed. A major portion of what's currently available is listed in this guide, including both primitive and higher-standard trails; some are barrier-free. Also included are listings for parks, viewpoints, water access (beaches, boat ramps, and docks), and campgrounds.

Most trail miles in San Juan County are on San Juan, Orcas, Lopez, and Sucia Islands, while shorter walks are available on at least a dozen others, including a number of marine state parks. Most are open only to foot traffic, while a few on each of the larger islands are open to mountain bikes. Orcas' Moran State Park and San Juan's American Camp provide the bulk of hiking opportunities in the county, though Sucia Island's lengthy trail system is noteworthy as well.

In Skagit County, most of the mileage is found on Fidalgo and Cypress Islands where thousands of acres have been set aside for conservation and recreation. On Fidalgo, trails on Community Forest Lands are mostly designated multiuse, some of which are open to motorcycles, which can be a little disconcerting to hikers (motorized trails were generally avoided in this guide). All trails on Cypress Island, on the other hand, are designated hiker-only. Some of Skagit's better beach walks are found on Guemes and Sinclair Islands. Only selected trails are listed in order to avoid redundancy with a soon-to-be-released Skagit County guide. However, some of the best hikes these islands have to offer are included here.

In Island County, Camano Island accounts for a few trails at Camano Island State Park, but Whidbey Island, due in part to its large size and substantial public tidelands, accounts for more hikes than any other island, including 20 of the 80 hikes listed in this guide. Most trails are found within five different state parks, most notably Deception Pass and Fort Ebey State Parks, and within Ebey's Landing National Historical Reserve. Whidbey is also one of the more outstanding areas on Washington's inland sea for beach walks, including many miles of wild shores below high eroding bluffs. Bluff hikes are unique—something like walking in a gorge, but with one wall missing.

Overall, it's clear that these three counties have a lot to offer in the way of trails and walkable beaches. Your local trail sleuth will find even more than is listed here. Time and space limitations for this first edition preclude listing everything, although other hikes may be added in the future. For all islands, most trails are on lands managed by Washington State Parks and the Washington Department of Natural Resources (DNR). The rest are generally spread across a number of city and county parks, nature reserves, and private open space areas. Beach walks are predominantly on publicly owned tidelands also managed by DNR.

Whaт's iN тHE works...

To someone new to the area or who doesn't get out on the trail much, it may seem like all our trail worries are over. Yet despite the sound of it, the overall trail system in the islands is far from complete. Perhaps the most obvious trail deficiencies are the general lack of high-quality hiking trails linking communities with regional trails, or with nearby parks and natural areas. There is also a deficit of urban trails and greenways in almost all of the more populated areas. Local park and recreation plans generally recognize that more trails are needed to serve not only growing populations, but the increasing popularity of trails generally.

Thanks to the dedication of concerned citizens, agency staff, and community leaders, plans have been developed in all three counties to address the need, and public demand, for more trails. Though funding is often a major obstacle for larger projects, there is no shortage of good ideas for future trails. In fact, in early 2001 San Juan County was embarking on a new effort to identify opportunities to expand on existing trails and bikeways throughout the region, but especially on the four main islands. Skagit County recently updated its park and recreation plan and its nonmotorized transportation plan to address bicycle and pedestrian needs regionwide.

Island County residents have demonstrated strong support for improving and expanding trails and bikeways on both Whidbey and Camano Islands, and significant improvements have been made in recent years. In a random household survey conducted in the mid-1990s, nearly half of Whidbey's residents indicated they use trails and beaches for hiking at least once a month, on average. A number of ambitious trail projects have already been identified, and with the help of grants, volunteers, and a supportive public, their development may be just around the corner.

The growing demand for trails raises at least three interesting questions: First, can we, as a society, afford to build and maintain an enjoyable and solidly interconnected regional trail systems? Perhaps we can't afford not to. If quality of life is something we want to keep around for awhile, trails must be an integral component in the ongoing development of our communities. Informal paths on private lands are rapidly disappearing, thus new opportunities for public access are sorely needed. And acquiring corridors for future trails will only get more complicated and expensive over time.

Second, does building more trails (or publishing more guidebooks, for that matter) only attract more trail users to fill them up and thereby diminish the quality of the trail experience? In a very limited way, perhaps. People may have to wander a little farther from home or farther from the trailhead to find solitude as more good people inevitably come to "our" trails, but the benefits seem to far outweigh the costs. People who walk on trails almost invariably find something valuable in the experience. It might be purely recreational, or personal, or spiritual, or educational, or whatever, but if people value the experience, there's a chance they will also value the place. And what we clearly need more of these days is more people who value place—whether it's an old-growth forest, an unpolluted lake, a quiet marsh, or a spectacular island vista. If trails take us to places that mean something to us, maybe we'll be inspired to take care of them.

Finally, can the natural environment withstand us all loving it to death simultaneously? Most likely not. We've seen the damage caused by overuse and abuse in rocky meadows where thin soils and dry summers tend to exaggerate the damage from trampling and other use. We hear plenty about the need to protect water quality around sensitive lakes and streams. Many of us have stopped to pick up other people's garbage along the trail, mystified by the mentality of those who might just as well trash the planet. We also know how humans can interfere with the needs of wildlife, some whose last refuge may be a single island wilderness in the San Juans.

Certainly we can't all rely on parks and wild places as one big happy playground dedicated to the weekend whims of humanity, nor should we presume that less pristine areas are any less sensitive to our numbers or our carelessness. Yet we can enjoy these areas as concerned individuals and learn to explore them in ways that keep them intact and unspoiled. We can learn to coexist with wildlife and the land. We can care about the *place*, and we can encourage others to do the same.

PROTECTING WILD PLACES

One morning in late March, sitting on a log in an Orcas Island cove, I watched the tide creep in, slowly erasing the previous evening's boot tracks in the fine gravel. It was early, but the day was already well underway. Kingfishers announced the sunrise with their squeaky nonstop rattling. A pair of eagles screeched finely above and out of sight, while red-breasted mergansers paddled and dipped their heads in the water just far enough to see breakfast. A gull spun large circles, hovered briefly, then dropped to the water beak first, the flash of a wriggle in its mouth as it took to the air again. Nuthatches buzzed in the woods amid the light chorus of kinglets. Crows crowed, a raven squawked. A song sparrow sang. A flicker drummed and harped for a mate. The winter wrens wrenned endlessly, and red robins carried on their long and deliberate morning conversation....

Obviously, the islands are much more than a pretty place for people to live and recreate. Hundreds of bird species depend on diverse habitats to feed, nest, and raise their young. Many mammals, reptiles, amphibians, fish, even insects depend on a healthy environment, just like we do. To ensure that these and all other species have a viable future ahead, a diversity of habitats must be protected from the impacts of people. The future of island ecosystems, particularly at the landscape level, depends on protecting much more land from development than we already have, especially as many more of us crowd ourselves into the same fields and forests. Where we do use the land for our own purposes, we will need to become increasingly sensitive to the needs of wildlife, or they will simply perish. It will not be enough to casually say we care, then go level the forest and plop down a house somewhere. We'll need to be vigilant in our commitments to both responsible development and wildlife conservation.

Fortunately, citizens and agencies in all three counties have made conservation and environmental protection high priorities on virtually every island. Leading the way are organizations like the **San Juan Preservation Trust** which in twenty years' time has helped protect thousands of acres in the islands, including 762 acres of Trust-

Little Matia Island

owned preserves, and conservation easements on more than 8,000 acres. From Guemes to San Juan Island, the Trust seeks to "preserve and protect open space, forests, agricultural lands, habitats, wetlands and shorelines" in the islands of San Juan and Skagit Counties. The Trust also sponsors lectures and tours to some reserves.

In 1990, San Juan County voters passed a ballot measure creating the **San Juan County Land Bank** and imposing a one percent transfer tax on every real estate transaction to go toward land acquisitions and conservation easements, with a portion of the funds set aside for stewardship. With county staff support, the program is overseen by a citizens committee, while volunteers help look after the sites that are acquired. By raising about $1.5 million each year, the Land Bank protects areas of scenic, recreational, agricultural, historic, cultural, or scientific importance, plus potable water sources. Their work was so successful—with almost 1,700 acres protected by 1998—and popular that voters extended the program in 1999 by nearly a three-to-one margin. Acquisitions have included lands adjacent to Lime Kiln Point State Park on San Juan Island, the Hummel Lake and Watmough Bay Preserves on Lopez Island, and a number of sites on Orcas Island and elsewhere.

The Nature Conservancy manages several reserves in the islands, including Yellow, Sentinel, Goose, and Deadman Islands, plus a 400-acre reserve on Waldron Island. Only Yellow Island is open to visitors (see Hike 80). The **San Juan Islands National Wildlife Refuge** protects 84 islands, rocks, and reefs totaling 454 acres, most of which are designated wilderness. Only Turn and Matia Islands are open to public use. The refuge safeguards habitat for gulls, cormorants, pigeon guillemots, tufted puffins, rhinoceros auklets, oystercatchers, eagles, and many shorebirds and marine mammals. Boaters must stay at least 200 yards offshore of these refuge islands.

The marine environment is also benefitting from the work of seven *Marine Resource Committees* (one for each county in the region) established under the 1998 Northwest Straits Marine Conservation Initiative. These citizen-based committees are working to restore marine habitats, improve shellfish areas, help with salmon and bottomfish recovery, and find ways to protect marine areas.

These are important efforts and we should all support them.

ACCESSING PARADISE

As noted earlier, the islands of San Juan, Skagit, and Island Counties can be accessed in various ways. Each entry in the guide includes basic information about the most likely modes of travel that may be involved, especially in reaching the more out-of-the-way places. Car ferries, foot-ferries, water taxis, private water craft, airplanes, and, in some cases, bridges are the usual means of accessing paradise. Bridges link the mainland to Camano, Whidbey, and Fidalgo Islands, so access to these islands is easiest. Public bus transit is available to these same islands, and includes stops at the San Juan, Guemes Island, Clinton–Mukilteo, and Keystone–Port Townsend ferry terminals (see below). Public transit is free in Island County. The more populated islands all have airstrips, while regular shuttle airline service may be available to Friday Harbor from Bellingham, Seattle, and other regional airports.

Car & foot ferries…

The vast majority of visitors to the San Juan Islands will simply drive onto the ferry at Anacortes and disembark at one of the four large islands served: Lopez, Shaw, Orcas, or San Juan. The Washington State Ferry System operates regular ferry service to each island several times a day, all year long, with a slightly extended schedule during the summer months. One boat daily continues on to Victoria, British Columbia. Fares and schedules vary and change seasonally, so call the automated ferry information line at (800) 843-3779 for up-to-the-minute information. Fares are charged only for west-bound travel between the islands. All San Juan Island ferries leave from the Anacortes ferry terminal 4.5 miles west of downtown.

The ferry system also serves two routes to and from Whidbey Island, including the Keystone–Port Townsend run west of Coupeville, and the Clinton–Mukilteo run near the south end of the island. Routes to the ferry terminals are well signed from I-5 and SR 20. Busy times are somewhat predictable; long waits are common on most summer weekends. Arrive at least an hour early to increase the odds of catching the boat you want. Fares are charged both directions on these routes. Skagit County also operates a small car ferry between Anacortes and Guemes Island, more or less hourly from early morning to early evening (later on Friday and Saturday nights). The trip is only about five minutes long. The ferry dock is located at I Avenue north of 6th Street. For Guemes ferry information, call (360) 293-6356.

Several private companies offer foot-ferry and water taxi service to the larger San Juan islands, as well as to many of the smaller outliers, either on a seasonal schedule or by arrangement. For more information, check the Web, travel information centers, or any of the major harbors, including Anacortes, Bellingham, Seattle, Friday Harbor, and elsewhere for more information. These services can be especially useful and cost-effective for group travel.

Boating in the islands…

Experienced boaters can probably find their own way to any of the sites listed in this guide, and in fact, should be able to do so proficiently, either through experience, information from others, or with the help of maps, charts, and various boating guides intended for that purpose. Again, this book is not a boaters guide, but rather a guide to walking and hiking opportunities available once you arrive on your island of choice. Nevertheless, basic information concerning boat access is provided for convenience. Additional information is sometimes provided for kayakers who can glide into places not always accessible to sailboats and motorboats.

For general boating safety information, the Washington Boating Safety Officers Association and U.S. Power Squadrons in the region offer information and boating safety short-courses—highly recommended for all boaters, whether you go by wind, motors, or brute force. Washington State Parks also publishes a free *Boaters Guide* that can be found at many of the larger state parks where boating is accommodated. See *Further Reading* in the back of the book for more good references on boating in the region.

Moorage & campsites…

The descriptions here also note the availability of mooring facilities and boating oriented campsites, many of which are found at marine state parks. Marine state parks are those generally accessed by boat only, such as Stuart, Sucia, Turn, and Jones Islands. Mooring buoys and anchorages are typically available at developed marine state parks, though not always in protected locations. Docks and seasonal floats are sometimes provided, with floats often being removed fall through early spring due to the beating they take during fall and winter storms. Fees are charged for overnight mooring or camping, and annual permits are available for frequent travelers. Fees can vary by boat length and the duration of stay. There is generally no charge to tie up to a dock or buoy for a brief daytime visit. Always adhere to boating safety rules and regulations, be courteous to others, avoid disturbing wildlife, and leave no trace of your visit (amazingly, some folks still need to be reminded).

Cascadia Marine Trail...

Of special interest to those traveling by kayak, canoe, or beachable sailboat, the Cascadia Marine Trail directs paddlers to marine parks and remote campsites throughout the islands, many in locations that are more difficult for other boaters to access. Users of the Cascadia Marine Trail can also pay for campsites either on a daily basis or by way of an annual pass. For more information or to obtain a pass, check the Washington Water Trails Association website at www.wwta.org, or write WWTA, 4649 Sunnyside Ave. No., Rm. 305, Seattle, WA 98103. Fees go toward maintenance and expansion of the water trail.

Walking & bicycling...

There is much to see and do in the islands that doesn't require a boat or a car, so consider walking or biking to the islands to avoid the long waits and increasing costs of visiting the islands by automobile. You can also find bicycle and moped rentals at most island urban centers and some resorts. The four larger islands of the San Juans are popular for cycling tours, Lopez and San Juan Islands in particular. Orcas Island's many hills and winding roads are more challenging than the other islands, while Shaw is small enough that most cyclists can complete a leisurely tour there in just a few hours and move on. Cycling on Guemes and Whidbey Islands is also a delight, while Camano Island can be downright scary at times (try to avoid the major thoroughfares). Whidbey is a big island with lots of backroads favorable to cycling, and much to see. Cycling guides and maps are available for all these islands. There are also bike-friendly campsites on most of the islands served by ferries or bridges.

Many bicyclists will drive to Anacortes, park, then bike onto the ferry. Logistically, the biggest concern is usually where to leave the car. There are several options. A large, fee-based parking area is available adjacent to the San Juan Islands ferry terminal, but when you add the cost of parking to the fare for biking onto the ferry, there is little or no incentive to leave the car behind. This is an unfortunate weakness of the state ferry system that only serves to increase the number of cars taking the ferry, rather than helping to reduce congestion by encouraging people to bike or walk on. This adverse pricing policy really ought to be revised. Meanwhile, the current "solution" consists of a free parking lot eight miles east of the ferry terminal (near the oil refinery), and a free, hourly shuttle that may or may not have room for your bicycle. The free shuttle works better without a bike in tow.

Bicyclists can ride the eight miles from the lot, but will have to contend with highway traffic along the way. Another solution for car-free folks is to park along the street in Anacortes and bike shorter distance to the ferry. For overnight trips, perhaps the best option is to leave a car in the overnight lot at Washington Park in Anacortes ($2 per night as of June 2001), then make the ten-minute ride to the terminal. This works quite well for adult riders. If kids are part of the plan, it may be best for the driver to drop everyone at the terminal first, then park the car and bike back to rejoin the group.

At the terminal, cyclists and pedestrians purchase tickets at the main building near the ferry dock. Cyclists walk between the fence and the building to proceed onto the ferry when directed by crew. You will be asked to secure your bike above the curbs at the front of the ferry (a bungee cord helps). Pedestrians use the overhead ramp to board unless otherwise directed. Bikes and foot traffic are first to load and first to off-load at each island, ahead of the cars (at least they got that part right). *Once you pay your fare to leave Anacortes, all further inter-island ferry travel is free if you are on bike or on foot.* Some resorts provide shuttle van service to and from the ferry dock once you are on the island. For those walking or cycling to Guemes Island, a small free parking area is provided next to the dock.

ABOUT THE ISLANDS

An icy, fiery past...

Continental glaciers, we know, imposed an enormous influence on the North American landscape over the past several hundred thousand years, shaping much of what we see today from southern Puget Sound to British Columbia and beyond. Ice sheets more than a mile thick buried the San Juan Islands, and much of the North Cascades and Olympic Mountains, finally melting and retreating for the last time less than 12,000 years ago. As the ice moved and strained across bedrock, the glacier's own rubble scraped innumerable striations in the rock that can easily be seen today in areas where smooth bedrock is exposed. Some of the rubble, known as glacial erratics (boulders), lie scattered about the region—rocks that don't match the bedrock they're sitting on.

Over several million years, what were once mountains 10,000 feet higher, have been reduced by glaciers and other erosive forces to mere hills partly submerged in the sea. Meanwhile tectonic plates have slipped and collided below, producing earthquakes and spawning volcanoes. Dominating the east horizon, Mount Baker, Washington's third highest volcano, last erupted in 1870 and can still be seen emitting steam from the fumaroles in its summit crater.

As the glaciers advanced and retreated, the melting ice and huge meltwater rivers dumped layers of sediment, sometimes hundreds of feet thick, over much of the lowlands of northwest Washington. These layers are evident in the high bluffs along the west shore of Whidbey Island and elsewhere. As the ice vanished and the climate moderated, vast forests gradually reclaimed the land. Wildlife, salmon, and humans moved into the region. The land, freed of this enormous burden of ice, went into rebound as if someone took 12,000 years to step off a 400-foot trampoline. But the sea also rose, fed by the melting continents.

Scientists can watch these natural processes over decades and lifetimes to extrapolate from their observations what most likely occurred over spans of time that most mortals can hardly fathom. Researchers help us see the natural landscape as the logical result of something dynamic and unshakeable, a sub-earthen waltz of entire continents drifting around the globe, as pieces of oceanic and continental crust collide almost imperceptibly in ultra slow-motion, and as volcanoes erupt through the weakened rock where one tectonic plate slides hotly beneath another. The not-yet-final results of all this geological commotion are places like those we now arbitrarily refer to as San Juan, Skagit, and Island Counties.

Island biodiversity...

In the "mountains" of the San Juans today, lakes, streams, waterfalls, forests, meadows, wetlands, rock outcrops, and hundreds of miles of marine coastline support rich and diverse ecosystems comprised of many familiar—and not-so-familiar—species. Inch-long Pacific chorus frogs liven up the evenings in early spring. An eighteen-inch northern alligator lizard shuffling over the rock can be a mildly startling sight for the uninitiated (they're generally harmless but can bite). In the cool shade of a damp forest, a rough-skinned newt can suddenly appear under your feet, well camouflaged against the trail. Little brown bats circle and dive for bugs at dusk. A 40-pound beaver may be heard slapping its tail on a marshy pond in the late afternoon. A newborn fawn may appear with its mother in a grassy meadow—or in the middle of the road—in spring. The flash of a shy red fox slipping into the woods is always a thrill. A pair of young river otters chasing each other along the rocky shore, tumbling down the rocks and into the water with a splash is a delight to watch, even if some waterfront residents find them a little pesky (there are no sea otters in the islands). Even tiny hermit crabs skittering around a rocky beach can pass for cheap entertainment just about anytime. Offshore, seals, leaping salmon, sea lions, orcas, and dozens of waterfowl species remind us of the great diversity found in the marine environment.

Island wildlife and the natural environment that is their habitat are also what make the islands so attractive and enjoyable to people—places to celebrate Northwest living. Spoil it as we may with our bulldozers, chainsaws, dynamite, concrete, steel, asphalt, trash, and effluent, much remains that is still well worth taking care of. To our good fortune, all three counties, various state and federal agencies, and even many private organizations and landowners have taken great steps to ensure that unspoiled areas and unique natural features remain intact for our generation and future generations to enjoy. These pieces of protected land—more than 25,000 acres worth—are home to the region's prized biodiversity.

The largest protected areas include nearly 5,000 acres of Natural Area Preserve and Natural Resource Conservation Area on Cypress Island; more than 2,000 acres of Community Forest Lands on Fidalgo Island; 5,000 acres of partly protected lands within Moran State Park; another 4,000 acres at Deception Pass State Park; 84 islands, rocks, and rock clusters within the San Juan Islands National Wildlife Refuge; plus at least 10,000 more acres of parks and reserves throughout the islands of all three counties. It may sound like a lot, but far more than that has been severely altered by development. In the islands, roadways alone occupy many thousands of acres. Thus the numbers can be deceiving. In a place as biologically rich as the islands, much more deserves to be protected.

Some prehistory...

Before Washington's first white settler landed on the north bank of the Columbia River in the 1820s, the Northwest was already home to at least hundreds of thousands of people—Native Americans who had lived, worked, played, hunted, fished, cultivated, and developed their own unique cultural traditions in the region over thousands of years. Many allied and competing tribes inhabited the Coast Salish region which includes the San Juan archipelago, though it is believed that most permanent villages were on the mainland, not on the islands. The islands were apparently valued more as summer and winter seasonal encampments, evidenced by the many middens, or shell heaps, found at sites revisited year after year for generations.

The Lummi Tribe and their ancestors are known to be among the those who made substantial use of the islands, as did several other tribes in the vicinity. Whidbey Island was apparently occupied by five different, mutually friendly, tribes when settlers arrived here in the 1840s. The Swinomish and Skagit lived to the north, while Snohomish and Suquamish people lived in the southern parts. And the Clallams were frequent visitors from the Olympic Peninsula.

The all-important cedar trees, plus abundant deer, salmon, shellfish, roots, and berries made for an easy and relatively peaceful subsistence, despite occasional bloody raids by tribes from farther north who were known to terrorize native communities throughout the region. These raids continued into the 1850s when many whites were targeted as well. Bloodshed was substantial on all sides. Yet the islands gave much to the native peoples, and through their stories and spiritual traditions they revered the gifts made available to them by the natural world. The natives at Cultus Bay on south Whidbey Island, an area particularly rich in clams, crabs, and huckleberries, even referred to the place as "Paradise."

At English Camp on San Juan Island, a walking tour brochure notes how native people simply appeared to have vacated their own camp in the area about the same time the British established a military camp to further Britain's claim to the San Juan Islands. Coincidence? Hardly. Settlers moving into the region in the 1850s uprooted native communities almost everywhere they went, at times forcibly. Diseases introduced by the newcomers took a heavy toll on tribal members whose immune systems knew no resistance to these alien infections. Violent and otherwise, the great upheaval experienced by native people over a few short decades in the mid-1800s still has not been thoroughly assessed.

Some History...

It must have been a remarkable event when a few Native Americans caught their first glimpse of a sailing ship appearing over the horizon in the Strait of Juan de Fuca. It is possible that Juan de Fuca himself, otherwise known as the Greek pilot, Apostolus Valerianos, did in fact sail into the strait in 1592. His records were weak, however, and have been doubted ever since. Nevertheless, others after him found the strait essentially where he reported it. American Captain Robert Gray almost reached the islands in 1789, but it was Spanish Lieutenant Francisco Eliza who led a 1791 expedition that resulted in the first detailed maps and a proliferation of Spanish place names within the island archipelago. Nearly all the Spanish names can be attributed to Eliza and his subordinate, Lopez Gonzales de Haro (the man credited with "discovering" the San Juans): San Juan, Lopez,

Orcas, Patos, Sucia, Matia, Fidalgo, Guemes, and Camano Islands, as well as Haro and Rosario Straits.

A year later, British Captain George Vancouver sailed into the strait and remapped and renamed some of what he found. He named Georgia Strait for King George III. San Juan Island was called Bellevue. Vancouver also spent a great deal of time mapping the mainland coast and naming places for those he felt deserved to be honored: Bellingham Bay, Mount Baker, Whidbey Island, and Possession Sound—the latter to commemorate Vancouver's claim to the region on behalf of the British crown (barely sixteen years after the American Colonies declared their independence). Ship's Master Joseph Whidbey had made the surprising discovery that the treacherous looking shore southeast of Rosario Head was not just a rugged cove, as Vancouver had assumed. Thus the largest island on the west coast of the lower forty-eight states would be named Whidbey, and the passage that made it an island, Deception Pass. On June 4th, 1792, King George III's birthday, Captain Vancouver officially took possession of the entire region and called it New Georgia. In his honor, the Captain's name would be affixed to a much larger island in British Columbia.

In the 1830s, Lieutenant Charles Wilkes and the United States Exploring Expedition arrived and again renamed much of the geography, thereby asserting the American claim to a disputed territory. Wilkes' emphasis on Navy commanders and fallen heroes from the War of 1812 is reflected in many island names, including Allan, Barnes, Blakely, Burrows, Clark, Decatur, Frost, Henry, Jones, Shaw (an underling of Decatur), Sinclair, Spieden, Stuart, and Waldron. Also named by Wilkes were Flattop (for its shape), Obstruction (it blocked the way between Blakely and Orcas), Skipjack (for a fish), and Goose (for a goose).

It seems odd that of all the islands in the San Juans, none retain indigenous names. Only Lummi and Samish Islands near the mainland offer a hint of a Native American influence. Lieutenant Eliza's name was immortalized with a small island off the south shore of Lummi in Whatcom County. One of the more unusual names in the islands is Friday Harbor, apparently named for an old Hawaiian sheepherder brought here by the Hudson's Bay Company, whose presence on San Juan Island laid the groundwork for the so-called "pig war" that would ultimately settle the boundary between the United States and Canada.

In the 1850s, as settlers spilled northward into the region, some came only to subsist, others to prospect for gold, to establish saw-mills, to fish, or to capitalize on others who were trying to do the same. The territorial seat of Olympia grew and prospered, and a network of communities sprang up all the way to Canada, linked by boats and a fledgling economy. With pioneers and fortune-seekers making their way into the forested frontier, conflicts arose between newcomers and virtually all native tribes in the lowland region, at times escalating into deadly violence. Military forts were established in many areas of western Washington, but from lessons learned in previous Indian wars of the West, a more concerted attempt at pacification, perhaps, led to the signing of the Point Elliot Treaty at Mukilteo in 1855. Territorial Governor Stevens, his delegation, a number of tribal chiefs, and 2,000 to 4,000 native people assembled for the occasion. In exchange for peace, a few scraps of reservation land, and guaranteed access to hunting and fishing grounds, the natives let go of a vast territory from Seattle to Canada. The treaty, unfortunately, has been repeatedly violated over the years, as much of the Indian land fell into non-native hands. Disastrous attempts were made to forcibly assimilate Native Americans into the white Euro-American culture, and the salmon catch, in particular, was unfairly distributed. (The famous Boldt decision in the 1970s helped rectify the latter.)

After Thomas Glascow, Whidbey Island's first settler, landed at Ebey's Prairie in 1848, hopeful immigrants from England, Ireland, Scandinavia, Holland, and elsewhere soon followed, during a time when the Haidas of the north were still raiding the islands' native villages in their giant war canoes. Colonel Isaac Ebey arrived in 1850 and staked the first official claim. On the Olympic Peninsula, Port Townsend was founded in 1851, and grew quickly to become an economic and communication lifeline for Whidbey Island. In 1853, Island County was established by the new territorial legislature, thanks in part to the efforts of Ebey, a prominent figure in Washington's fledgling territorial government, who would ultimately lose his head to the Haidas in retaliation for an American ambush. Coveland—at the head of Penn Cove—was the first county seat, though it was later moved to sea captain Thomas Coupe's little dream town of Coupeville. An 1853 census counted 170 non-natives in all of Island County. In 1855 there were 1,500 Native Americans on Whidbey alone. Island County originally included what we know today as Island, San Juan, Skagit, and Whatcom Counties, but just a year later, the legislature split the area in two and Whatcom County, which included the San Juans, was born.

Following arrival of the Hudson's Bay Company and its salmon processing and sheep-raising operations on San Juan Island in the early 1850s, both Americans and the British began settling in the islands in small numbers—a region whose sovereignty was still in dispute because of poor language in a territorial treaty with England. The strait between Vancouver Island and the mainland had previously been agreed to as a boundary, but in reality there were two straits, Haro and Rosario, with the San Juans sandwiched between. The dispute came to a head on San Juan Island when a British-owned pig rooted in an American's garden and the garden's owner shot it. A simple event became an international incident as both sides flexed their political muscles, and installed military encampments—British Camp and American Camp—to assert their respective jurisdictions. Germany's Wilhelm I arbitrated a settlement and the San Juans were ultimately awarded to the Americans in 1872. A year later, San Juan County agitators succeeded in having themselves split off from Whatcom, after the authorities in Bellingham tried to impose a new tax on personal property. Only 200 settlers—they didn't count the wives and kids—lived in the new county, mostly on San Juan Island, and a few on Orcas and Lopez.

Beginning around 1880, Chinese immigrants arrived (or were smuggled) in large numbers, providing low-cost labor to employers and landowners from Canada to California. In just a few years significant Chinese communities of laborers had emerged on San Juan Island and central Whidbey Island, where many white settlers expressed grief over declining wages and a poor job market that resulted from large pools of Asian men willing to do good work for low pay. Potatoes harvested with cheap labor were mysteriously

English Camp, San Juan Island

dynamited, and rogue bullets sailed through Chinese homes.

In 1886, John McMillin bought the houses and lime kilns at Roche Harbor and turned the operations into a thriving money-maker. Three years later, Robert Moran, of Rosario fame on Orcas Island, was elected mayor of Seattle, having arrived there fourteen years earlier as a poor, young job-seeker from New York. He would soon become a wealthy industrialist. When he was diagnosed with a serious heart problem, he moved to Orcas, built Rosario, and became one of the state's most prominent philanthropists. Moran State Park would later become his best-known gift to the people of Washington.

By the 1890s, railroads were spreading across the mainland, while a "Mosquito Fleet" of steamships made frequent runs from Seattle to Bellingham, stopping at Clinton, Langley, Coupeville, Oak Harbor, La Conner, Anacortes, and elsewhere. Only ten years earlier, whites would often hire a half-dozen natives to paddle them in their large canoes to the mainland in order to pick up supplies and collect the mail. A canoe trip from Whidbey to Olympia might take a week-long round trip. Steamboats and railroads brought new and dramatic changes. The steamship run from Seattle to Oak Harbor was reduced to only seven hours. Ships grew bigger and faster, and some could carry 1,000 people or more, with full-course meals and piano music for entertainment. Developers prepared to dig a canal across the narrow neck of Whidbey Island at Ebey's Prairie to shorten the trip for Seattle to Victoria ships. Then, almost as suddenly as it began, the immensely successful steamship era vaporized with the massive development of internal combustion engines and an expanding regional road system that literally paved the way for automobiles to take control of the once vastly forested landscape of the Northwest. By 1912, the first car ferry had bridged the gap at Deception Pass.

To better defend these prosperous shores at the turn of the century from real or perceived threats, defense installations were constructed at Fort Worden near Port Townsend and Fort Casey on Whidbey Island, equipped with 12-inch guns that could lodge a 1,000-pound shell over three miles. At the same time, in the spirit of peace and cooperation, Freeland was established on south Whidbey Island as a socialist colony, building on the successes and failures of its predecessor at Bow, up in Skagit County. The ideals of equality and prosperity for all were laudable, but relationships in a leaderless world became difficult to master. The concept was eventually abandoned, and the communities faded into more conventional towns. Throughout the islands, farming, sawmills, fish canneries, lime kilns, and real estate development fueled local economies.

There were difficult times, to be sure, particularly after WWI. Economies strained under local and national influences. A terrible fire destroyed much of downtown Oak Harbor in 1920. Also in the 1920s, during Prohibition, rum-runners found the islands a smugglers paradise and risked arrest, prison, hijackings, capsizing, thievery, murder, and mayhem to transport their precious cargo from Canada southward. But when times were tough in the Depression years, plenty of seafood, deer, and homegrown meat and vegetables eased the hard times considerably. F. D. R.'s Civilian Conservation

Corps went to work at Deception Pass and elsewhere to build many of the outstanding park facilities we still enjoy today. In July 1935, the Deception Pass Bridge opened. In the same period, a relative of Bing Crosby put together a popular ferry run through the San Juan Islands, the precursor to today's state-run ferry service. In the 1940s, the Whidbey Naval Air Station began as an airfield where Clover Valley had been cleared by Dutch farmers fifty years before. Until 1942, Oak Harbor had no paved streets.

In 1961, Whidbey writer, Trudy Sundberg, described the island as a place to see "double rainbows... no parking meters... a boat in every other garage...," and where "men go home for lunch" and strangers say "Here, take these ducks." Soon enough, however, the 'burbs of Seattle and mainland Puget Sound began to expand outwardly into the islands, as view properties were suddenly in hot demand. In the 1970s, San Juan County was the fastest growing county in Washington, leveling off somewhat (to 8,900 people) in the mid-1980s. Also by the 1970s, oil refineries had landed on Fidalgo Island in response to oil and gas development in Alaska.

Yet the islands have otherwise remained free of large-scale industrial development. An aluminum smelter proposed for Guemes Island in the 1960s was stopped cold by public opposition, despite the strong support of Skagit County boosters. The battle raised awareness regionally about the threats of development to island living and the natural environment. Nevertheless, new homes have appeared by the thousands over the past two decades, and tourism continues to grow, as travelers from around the world discover the many scenic jewels of the Northwest, and Washingtonians head out in ever-greater numbers to explore their own backyards. At the same time, small agricultural operations have remained viable on many islands, while cottage industry, marine and small-town services, and the arts continue to thrive as critical elements of a regionally sustainable economy.

THE FUTURE...

Although development has been somewhat limited by the inherent isolation of island living, the islands are not immune to growth. In the 1990s, Skagit, Island, and San Juan Counties were among the fastest growing places in the state. San Juan County has now surpassed 14,000 residents, with half of them living on San Juan Island. On a typical August day, tourists boost the county population by more than sixty percent, and in a year can bring tens of millions of dollars into the local economy. Median age is almost ten years older than the state as a whole, which helps keep the birth rate extremely low, thus growth is almost entirely from immigration, including many retirees. Oddly enough, average income in the San Juans is higher than that for the whole state, but wages paid are among the state's lowest. Anacortes, Oak Harbor, and Friday Harbor have generally grown as fast as the counties as a whole. Continued growth throughout western Washington further increases the pressure for more development in the islands.

Anyone who has watched this growth take place over the past two decades can scarcely fathom what might transpire over the next two decades. Growth and development are still going strong regionally. The state's hotly debated Growth Management Act is a potent law that is supposed to help by ensuring orderly and efficient growth while protecting critical natural areas from being destroyed. Yet at the rate new subdivisions and shopping centers have been replacing farms, fields, and forests on the mainland and in the islands, one can only wonder how or when it might possibly stop.

In the meantime, it is not just the infrastructure, or the pains of growth, politics, and economics that define the island region. It is the extraordinary coastlines, lakes, wetlands, streams, rivers, waterfalls, wooded foothills, old-growth forests, farms, meadows, urban centers, rural hamlets, and communities of Northwesterners living here that define this magnificent archipelago of islands called the San Juans. The uncertainty is how long we can keep it that way.

What to Know Before You Go

Climate & season...

The Olympic Mountains are so effective at stripping moisture from marine air blowing in from the Pacific that more than 100 inches of rain falls in an average year west of Mount Olympus, the high point of the range. More than fifteen feet of precipitation has been recorded in a single year, thanks to a few extra low-pressure systems continually streaming in from Alaskan waters. Yet, only a few miles to the east along the inside coast of the Olympic Peninsula and nearby islands, rainfall amounts drop considerably, in some places almost to semi-arid levels. The explanation is simple: moist air moving in from the sea cools and condenses as it rises over the mountains, producing large amounts of rain, then warms and expands as it descends down the eastern slopes and across the straits, gathering more moisture. Again, the air rises to pass over the North Cascades, producing more rain for western Washington, in progressively larger amounts as the elevation increases. This predominant pattern repeats itself many times throughout the year, but especially from November through March when 70 percent of annual precipitation falls. In summer, a warm Pacific High replaces the Aleutian Low and can change things dramatically. Rainfall amounts plummet and the sun may shine for weeks (a sunny stretch of two days or more is sure to keep a smile on most Northwesterners).

The San Juan Islands as well as Whidbey and even southern Vancouver Island all benefit from the rainshadow effect of the mountains. Most areas in the San Juans and Whidbey receive 20 to 30 inches of rain per year, compared to 35 to 60 inches annually at low elevations on the mainland to the east. While much of the annual precipitation in the Olympicss falls in winter as snow, lower elevations and warmer temperatures make snowfall in the islands a relatively rare occurrence, with the exception of Mount Constitution on Orcas Island. At 2,407 feet, the summit is high enough to collect a few feet of snow in winter, though it generally doesn't last.

Temperatures in the islands are just as comfortable as those on the mainland from late spring to early fall, and just as shivering, depending on your disposition, the rest of the year. Warm temperatures in the 70s and 80s can be expected during fair weather from May through September, dipping 10 to 20 degrees under gray skies, then becoming somewhat cooler the rest of the year. Even in winter, the weather is mild overall, but freezing conditions can occur on cold, clear days and nights.

For boaters, wind and fog are important weather concerns as well. Wind is funneled around islands, through the straits and passes, up and over hills and ridges, and out through the channels. This means that windspeed and direction can change quickly over short distances, and sometimes from one minute to the next. Stiff winds to twenty knots or more are fairly common in the straits all year long, while fall and winter storms sometimes kick up hurricane-force winds. Even sustained low-velocity winds will churn up sub-stantial waves and swell in open water, while rough conditions are common in more confined areas, especially when the wind is blow-ing against a tidal current. Wind poses one of the most serious threats to kayaks and other small boats due to the risk of capsizing. At the same time, the complexity of the islands' geography leaves many areas on the leeward side, protected from the wind, and boaters will seek them out, sometimes religiously. On the trail, wind is usually no more of a hindrance in the islands than anywhere else, although the warmth of the sun can fade oh-so-quickly as an afternoon breeze rudely invades your particular stretch of beach.

Prolonged periods of foggy weather are uncommon, but fog does occur, particularly in late summer. Fog typically dissipates by late morning or early afternoon. Of course, any time visibility is obscured, mariners should take precautions. Thousands of rocks, reefs, and shoals present a threat to the lost and ill-prepared.

Needless to say, the weather can be as fast-changing as it is unpredictable, so good raingear and warm clothing layers are es-sential. Sequential days of cold rain or gusty winds can be expected anywhere, anytime, with or without warning. Thunder storms oc-casionally occur, so avoid ridge tops, taller trees, and open water if you think lightning may strike in the vicinity. Requisite warnings stated, conditions in the islands are usually much more stable in summer than at other times. For the latest weather predictions, check the local forecast. Some news-radio stations provide fairly current reports, but some of the best weather information is broadcast via 24-hour VHF marine weather radio, as any Northwest boater would know. In the San Juans, we have the additional advantage of accessing weather reports from both U.S. and Canadian agencies, easily tuned in with the press of a button. Or check the weather on the Web at http://weather.noaa.gov/pd/waframes.html.

The mild temperatures and dry weather in the islands makes them accessible and worth exploring throughout the seasons. A spring saunter through the wildflower meadows of Mount Finlayson on San Juan Island is a perfect precursor to a midsummer trek to the alpine flowers of the Olympics and Cascades. A stormy fall day can be a great time for a little jaunt to Point Colville on Lopez Island to watch the pounding surf roll in from the Strait of Juan de Fuca. And the view from the summit of Fidalgo Island's Mount Erie on a cold clear day in January can be quite special. Summer, of course, is when most of us don the boots and hit the trails—be it in the mountains or the islands. For those of us who thrive on mountain hiking in the summer, the islands offer a perfect destination for the rest of the year, when the higher places are snowed in. On the islands in summer there also are far fewer people hanging around the trailheads.

Tides & currents...

For beach wanderers and the small-craft boaters among us who wish to explore some of the out-of-the-way places noted in this guide, a basic understanding of—and fundamental respect for—tides and currents is critical. Tides around the San Juan Islands, as most of us know, generally rise and fall twice a day, resulting in the two "highs" and two "lows" predicted in a common tide table. Each day, one of the highs is higher than the other and one of the lows is lower. The highest and lowest tides occur during a new or full moon, at which times the elevation difference between the higher high tide and the lower low tide can exceed ten feet. Obviously, boaters need to be aware of these changes so they don't run aground.

Changing tides also spell a warning to coastal hikers who may wander along a seemingly high and dry beach, only to find themselves clambering through brush and trees two hours later, finding the beach submerged. The highest tides can be downright dangerous below steep, eroding bluffs; and during stormy weather, tides may run higher than called for in the tables. Always commit to a turn-around time (or an escape route) before proceeding on a hike in these conditions. Every visitor to the coastal world should at least invest in a tide table, widely available in outdoor shops, bookstores, boating supply stores, and even supermarkets.

With such an enormous volume of water moving in and moving out (flooding and ebbing) through the straits with each high and low tide, strong currents can form in almost every channel or passage, as well as in shallow areas, where a large amount of water is forced through a constricted space. Currents in excess of two to three knots (*1 knot = approximately 1.15 miles per hour*) are quite common. At Deception Pass, notorious for its rapid tidal currents, speeds frequently exceed eight knots. A speed boat can often zip along against that much current, but a sailboat or kayak has to struggle to make any headway at all against even a three-knot current (most kayakers try to avoid paddling against more than one knot). Sometimes the flood (rising) tide will produce faster currents than the ebb (falling) tide, and sometimes not. If you look at a map and imagine the water flowing in and out of Juan de Fuca Strait, it's easy to understand why the flood tides generally flow north and east through the islands, while the ebbs tend to flow south and west. There are many exceptions, however, and in some cases the flood and ebb both flow in the same direction! Don't wing it. If safety depends on it, check the maps and tables before your trip.

Because the tides are driven by the constant force of gravity of the sun and moon, they are fairly predictable, thus so are the currents. Current tables and charts have been developed for boaters which give a clear indication, hour-by-hour, of the general speed and direction of currents. What these broad predictions cannot address are very localized conditions that can be far more serious than indicated on any chart. For example, circling eddies like those in a river will often form along the shores of channels, and tide rips—choppy or breaking waves in fast water—present an additional hazard of special concern to kayakers. Paddling from an eddy into a strong current, or vice-versa, can turn one's world upside down in a hurry. Those rowing a skiff or dinghy are vulnerable to similar threats, but since their mother ship is more likely to be anchored in a more calm and protected place, the dinghy rower is not generally as exposed to the elements as a kayaker crossing a channel.

Again, this is not a boaters guide. However, it is important to emphasize some of the challenges that await those without much experience who may be contemplating a "quick trip" to any of the places listed in this guide. There are plenty of how-to/where-to resources available for beginning boaters, including books, videos, classes, guided trips, and firsthand advice from seasoned San Juan mariners. Check with your local Coast Guard office for information on a boaters safety course. These resources are there to be taken advantage of. Do it, stay safe, and wear a life jacket.

Cold water & hypothermia...

Capsizing in our inland sea would not be such a worry if Washington was in the tropics and everyone wore life jackets. But one toe in the saltwater here should be enough to explain why so few people go swimming in the pretty coves and bays in summer. Winter to summer water temperatures vary between the mid-40s to low-50s, which is cold enough to bring on *hypothermia, unconsciousness, and drowning within a half an hour of going overboard*. By wearing a life jacket, assuming a fetal position, and not flailing around losing heat and energy unnecessarily, survival times might be extended to one or a few hours. If a current is carrying you away from shore, an hour might well be an eternity. Wet and dry suits can help tremendously, but are less comfortable in warm weather and are not often worn, even though the experts may recommend them.

On the trail, hypothermia is still a concern, like on cold wet days that started out warm and sunny. Hikes in the islands tend be less committing than those in the mountains, which generally means easier access to a warm space and a cup of hot tea when the weather deteriorates. On the other hand, a trip to one of the more remote areas in this guide could really test your mettle if you somehow ended up with wet clothes and no spares on a chilly day. Hypothermia (i.e., exposure) has claimed the lives of more than a few unprepared victims. Use good common sense. If you're dressed for the weather, hiking season in the islands can, indeed, last all year.

Preparation...

A rewarding trip is usually one with good preparation: proper dress and footwear, adequate food and water, and a few other basic items in the rucksack. For boaters, *carry and use an approved personal flotation device*, otherwise known as a PFD or life jacket, as well as any other items pertinent to your mode of travel. If you don't know what they are, you shouldn't be out there.

More advice: tell someone where you're going and know your limits. Anticipate problems that might arise and prepare for them. Is the weather unstable? When does it get dark? When does the tide come in? What time was that last ferry, anyway?

This guide is not intended to prepare you for overnight back-packing trips—though a few of the hikes listed, like those at Moran State Park, offer great overnight possibilities. Consult the library, sporting goods stores, outdoor clubs (listed at the end of the book) and knowledgeable persons if you want to further your skills in wilderness camping and other backcountry adventures. Numerous books are available that provide very specific information on clothing, equipment, navigation, camping, weather, hazards, and other elements with which you may unfamiliar.

Clothing & Equipment...

A suggested clothing and equipment list is provided below. Wear comfortable, loose-fitting layers that can be added or removed as necessary. Just being fashionable won't do. Under typical Northwest skies, the best combination in cool weather often includes a fast-drying synthetic layer against the skin, a light wool shirt or sweater, durable pants (avoid cotton), a heavy, wool sweater or pile jacket, a wind and water-resistant shell (top and bottom), gloves or mittens, and a warm hat. Feet need special attention. On longer hikes, good-fitting boots or lightweight trail shoes are mandatory. Thick socks over thin may help absorb friction away from the skin.

Wet clothes, especially denim and other cotton fabrics, can contribute to a rapid and dangerous loss of body heat (whereas wool still insulates even when wet). Add layers, gloves, hat, and parka in colder weather. With some summertime exceptions, nights in the islands are usually cool or cold. A wool hat that pulls down over the ears makes a great thermostat. Put it on before you start shivering and remove it before you sweat or overheat. Effective, fashionable sunglasses with UV protection, and sun cream (SPF 15 or better) are appropriate for bright days, especially on the water.

For short day trips, a waist or fanny pack may be useful to carry food and drink, a nature guide, tide table, camera, windbreaker, and other items listed below. In remote areas, don't get caught in darkness or bad weather without the essentials in your rucksack. Study the following list and notice what other experienced hikers carry with them. For those who may be "hiking" by wheelchair (let's hear it for accessible trails), modify the list as needed.

Short walks: Food, water, proper clothing, footwear, camera, binoculars, guidebook, sunglasses, sun cream.

Short hikes: Same as above, plus sturdy trail shoes or lug-soled boots, small pack, extra clothing (sweater, raingear), pocket knife, whistle, flashlight, batteries, first-aid kit.

Longer dayhikes: Same as above, plus extra food, water, more clothes and raingear, map and compass (learn to use them), matches, fire-starter, foam pad, TP, insect repellent, emergency shelter.

Backcountry sanitation...

Cleaning and washing should always occur well away from water sources. Use common sense if you need to make a nature call where no facilities are available. Get well off the trail and 100 feet or more from streams and water bodies. Dig a shallow hole, then cover it well with soil, rocks, and sticks. Pack out your toilet paper, along with any other trash or recyclables. Never discard anything but body waste in a pit privy or composter outhouse. Composting toilets have become common in almost all the more popular parks in the islands.

Conditioning...

The better shape you're in, the more enjoyable the hiking will be, and the best way to get in shape may be (surprise!) to go for a hike. If you hike often, each trip should better prepare you for the next. The going should get easier as you improve your conditioning. Most trips described here require only average physical condition. To cover more miles while avoiding burnout, maintain a comfortable pace. Check with your doctor if you have any doubt about your ability to make the trip. If you're not in the greatest shape, start with the shorter hikes described and slowly work up to more strenuous hikes. Don't push yourself to the point that you are gasping for air or listening to your pulse pound in your head. Hiking is supposed to be fun. Take plenty of breaks, relax, and enjoy nature.

Some rules & precautions...

On arrival at the trailhead in parks and reserves, check with the ranger or information kiosks for regulations, trail conditions, and other details. Just because a hike is included in a book doesn't mean it will be totally safe. Conditions can change dramatically in a short period of time. So prepare well, and turn back if trail conditions or the weather seriously deteriorate. Keep your party size small, preferably six or less (no more than twelve); practice "no-trace" hiking and camping; don't trample vegetation by camping on it or short-cutting trails; pack out your garbage; control your pet (they're banned in certain areas); camp only in designated campsites; and avoid building fires outside of designated areas, especially in meadows or dry forest. Carry a small backpack stove if cooking is required. Beware of changing conditions and unseen hazards. Stay on the trail and don't lose it. If you do get lost, call out, stay put, and/or mark your location so it's visible from the air.

Fire...

Fire is a special concern on the islands. A small island could be quickly devastated by fire. In some areas it may be impossible to combat or dampen a fire before it endangers people or property. Even when fire-fighting help is readily available the damage can be severe, to people and the environment. We are learning to let wildfires burn in larger wildland ecosystems, but on the islands, much more is at risk. In campgrounds where fires are allowed, douse them cold before you leave, even if it's raining.

Water...

Another unique concern for the islands is water. At all times, bring your own. With few lakes, springs, or perennial streams to draw from, water is a scarce commodity in the San Juans. Everywhere you go, you are likely to see reminders to conserve. Use only what you need, and never leave a tap running unnecessarily. When driving to the islands, it doesn't hurt to keep an extra gallon in the trunk. Always boil or filter stream and lake water.

Emergencies & first aid...

Accidents, criminal activity, fires, lost hikers, and the like should be reported to local emergency officials, or simply call 911. Search and rescue activities are coordinated through the county sheriff, or U.S. Coast Guard for boating incidents. Call 911 or the sheriff if you need help with an injured party, or to report an overdue hiker or boater. Forest fires can be reported to 911, to DNR at (800) 562-6010, or to the local park ranger. For non-emergency related inquiries, contact the appropriate land management agency for the area.

When traveling in remote places, some knowledge of first aid is highly recommended, even essential. Take a basic first-aid and CPR course, and carry a small first-aid kit. Keep dry and exercise lightly if needed to stay warm.

Wildlife sightings...

If you happen to be lucky enough to see an unusual or uncommon animal, or any animal in distress, you should consider reporting the sighting to the nearest park ranger, wildlife official, reserve manager, or wildlife rehabilitation center. Marine mammal sightings, such as whales, orcas, sea lions, etc., can be phoned to the Marine Mammal Sightings Hotline at (800) 562-8832.

Dangerous creatures...

In terms of ferocious critters in the islands, about the worst you can expect from an unhappy wildlife encounter is a pilfered lunch or a gnawed hole in a pack or a tent from a small rodent or squirrel. A pesky raccoon can spoil your day by going after your food since they often associate humans with food. When camping, hang your food and trash and hope they can't reach it. There are no bears or dangerous snakes in the islands. You might be lucky enough to stumble across an alligator lizard, which can bite, but they really won't want much to do with you, even if their large size (over a foot long) seems a little threatening.

The most dangerous creature you may ever run into is the two-legged kind, but even such human troublemakers are fairly rare in these parts. If the worst happens (it rarely, rarely does) and you are confronted by a trouble-making nutcase on the trail, try to stay cool. Trust your instincts. Attract someone's attention; scream, run, or fight back as good old common sense dictates. To reduce the risk, don't travel alone. Report any criminal activity to the proper authorities, and/or call 911 if there's an emergency. Fortunately, violent crime seldom occurs on the trail (I have neither experienced a violent offense on the trail nor ever known anyone who has in thirty years of hiking in Washington).

All in all, there are far more friendly and benign critters in the wild to be appreciated than there are creatures to be feared. So, be wise—not paranoid—and enjoy the trip.

Insects...

Finally, the most hideous and terrifying wilderness creatures of all: bugs. Actually, bugs aren't bad at all. Bugs are great. Rather, it's their bites and stings that can spoil an otherwise perfect outing. For more sensitive folks (you probably know who you are), stings can be dangerous and may require immediate care (check with your doctor before hiking if you are worried). However, for most of us, bug bites are just part of the outdoors package. The worst stings tend to be from yellow jackets. They nest in rotten stumps and logs or holes in the ground, or in hanging paper nests. Once disturbed, they are amazingly quick to react. Still, you're unlikely to disturb a nest if you stay on the trail. Mosquitos, flies, and no-see-ums are usually active only during early mornings and early evenings in summer. Find a breezy place to relax, use a little jungle juice (citronella is much less poisonous than DEET, but might have to be applied more often), or try moving a few hundred yards away from moist areas. Skip the mosquito netting when hiking the San Juans. Unlike the Cascades and Olympics in early summer, bugs in the islands are generally sparse and quite tolerable anytime.

Hantavirus...

One other pesky life form we're supposed to worry about now is *hantavirus*, a rare but deadly malady carried primarily by some deer mice. When someone comes into contact with an infected rodent, say, by disturbing or sleeping near it's nest, it's possible to inhale tiny airborne bits of mouse urine, saliva, or feces which could then cause the occurrence of *hantavirus* pulmonary syndrome. By 1998, twenty-two cases had been confirmed statewide, including two in Snohomish County and one in San Juan County. Close to forty percent of the incidents were fatal: as fever, chills, muscle aches, and other flu-like symptoms develop within one to four weeks of contact, then rapidly turn into severe respiratory distress. Deer mice, the principal carriers, are about six to seven inches long to the tip of the tail and have a cute white belly and feet. Prevention is the key. Avoid the mice and their nests, as well as crude cabins, shelters, or other enclosed areas that may be infested or which are not well ventilated, and consider sleeping in a tent rather than on bare ground. Keep food and utensils sealed and protected from rodents. While the odds of contracting the illness are remote in Washington, reducing risk of exposure to a minimum isn't a bad idea.

SPEAK OUT...

Finally, take the time to learn about the natural environment of the islands. Bring your natural history guide to the wildflowers rather than the other way around. Exercise respect for other walkers, wildlife, and the environment. At home, take time on occasion to speak up for trails and wilderness. Before you and I arrived on the scene, others were doing that for us.

PRIVATE PROPERTY...

Veteran hikers may notice that some favorite trails are not included in the book. This is not because the author overlooked them necessarily, but rather because they may traverse private lands whose owners might not wish to advertise their use by the general public. Fear of liability for injuries, and threat of vandalism and fires are common concerns (although landowners are well protected from liability by state law). Local residents and fellow hikers are likely sources to consult in locating these semi-secret places and ascertaining what use is appropriate.

Some areas under private ownership have been made available through public access agreements, conservation easements and the like. At the same time, some conservation easements exclude recreational use in order to protect sensitive wildlife. Where such areas are open to the public, obey all signs, closed gates, fences, seasonal fire closures, or other indications that your presence is not welcome. Obtain permission where necessary. *Descriptions in this guide should not be construed as permission to violate private property rights.* Also, always assume that camping and campfires are not permitted outside of designated sites.

As for your own private property—your personal valuables, that is—don't leave them in your car. Trailhead theft in the islands is not as severe as in some other areas, but thieves do have a habit of showing up at the oddest hours to break a window and make off with your goods. Report thefts to the authorities.

Beach access...

It is often assumed that all beaches are open to the public. That is generally true in Hawaii, Oregon, and other coastal states, but it is not so cut and dried in Washington. Regrettably, the state sold off its best tidelands around our inland sea to private interests over much of this century. Not only was it an absurd thing to do, it left us with major difficulties in finding good access to more than a fraction of the region's spectacular coastline. The practice was banned about 30 years ago, but the damage was done. However, there is still a legal argument—and the author agrees—that the public never gave up its right (i.e., the public trust) to use tidelands to access public waters, whether for commerce or recreation, even though the mud and the crud may belong to an adjacent landowner. At least one county (Snohomish) has taken the position that "the tidelands may still be used for public access including trails—provided no other activities are included in the process that would infringe on the private property owner's other uses of the land." All that said, private property still deserves respect.

The vast majority of tideland owners are not snobs and couldn't care less whether you and I go for a harmless stroll along a remote beach. However, a few individuals who abuse the privilege. Obnoxious behavior, littering, and vandalism are primary concerns, especially where waterfront homes are located close to shore. Fortunately, remote, undeveloped areas are more interesting to visit and responsible hikers will encounter few problems with anxious landowners. On all beaches (public and private) use common sense:

don't start fires, be quiet, avoid hiking in large groups, respect wild-life and the marine environment, smile and be courteous to residents, and stay off the stairs and pathways leading up to their yards.

Beach walks may be good year-round, except during stormy periods. The suggested hikes in coastal areas may include both public and private tidelands and all have been used regularly by the public in the past, although it would take a title company and a survey crew to know for sure which areas are public. *Where tidelands are private, it is the user's responsibility to obtain prior authorization if necessary.* Visit during lower tide levels (check the tide tables), and be aware of rising tides which can surprise, strand, or drown you if you're not careful. *Walk these and all other areas at your own risk!*

HOW TO USE THIS BOOK

To make best use of this guidebook, first read the introductory material and **What to Know Before You Go**. Check the **Trail Locator Map** up front for possibilities. Hikes are arranged somewhat geographically on each island, though the islands are listed alphabetically for quick reference. A brief introduction is provided which may include important seasonal or access information. In the table of contents, hikes have been marked with 🥾 symbols to indicate their relative difficulty. Walks with one 🥾 symbol generally require less than an hour round trip, may cover as little as a half mile, and are not particularly steep or difficult. Hikes with three 🥾 🥾 🥾 symbols are more strenuous but vary greatly in length, steepness, and overall difficulty. Of course, what may seem for one person to be an easy stroll may be a real workout for the next. Round-trip distances (to one or more destinations), approximate time recommended, elevation gain, and directions from the nearest town or highway are provided. Estimated times are loosely gauged for walking speeds of one to two miles per hour. Three miles per hour is a brisk pace, and four is almost a trot, difficult to maintain over much distance. Additional time is added if there is much elevation gain. Always read the trail description for more details on the times and distances.

Following the hike descriptions is a list of public parks, viewpoints, water access, and campgrounds which briefly describes the location and facilities available, and may include short walks not listed elsewhere in the guide. All maps in this book are intended only for general reference, not for navigation. Far better, full-sized topographical maps and marine charts to all areas are available at many outdoor shops and boating supply outlets. USGS maps are useful for some hikes, but local park and trail maps, where they exist, often provide more detail and are usually the better choice.

Hiking the San Juan Islands is the only guide with broad coverage of the entire group of islands in the northern waters of Washington's inland sea, from the saltwater shore to the meadowy crest of Mount Constitution.

Several local outdoor clubs, environmental groups, and park and recreation entities sponsor guided hikes throughout the year, usually free of charge for members. These are also listed at the end of the book, along with emergency contacts and various land management agencies. Libraries, outdoor shops, and resource agency staff are other excellent sources of how-to/where-to hiking information. In the cyber world, the Washington Trails Association maintains an excellent Web site (www.wta.org) loaded with useful hiking information, mostly oriented to the mountains.

Get involved in trails...

If you enjoy using trails, consider giving something back to the community on occasion. Call or write your representatives in Olympia or the other Washington to encourage them to support trails and parks programs, or to donate time or money to a local trail education or maintenance program. San Juan, Skagit, and Island Counties offer many opportunities to work on trails. Call them for information about volunteer opportunities, upcoming projects, or how to connect with other trails organizations. To learn more about volunteering for trail work, contact the Washington Trails Association or Volunteers for Outdoor Washington (listed in the back of the book). You may be surprised by how enjoyable this kind of work can be. Volunteering is a fine way to get plugged into the local trail scene, pick up some hard-to-find trail information, discover new places, and maybe meet a new hiking partner or two.

Hiking the San Juan Islands

Hikes & Walks in San Juan, Skagit & Island Counties

Blakely Island

San Juan County

Fronting on Rosario Strait in the eastern San Juans, Blakely Island is the largest island in San Juan County that does not have regular ferry service, though it does have a marina and small airport. Much of the island is wooded and fairly wild, and two of the largest lakes in the San Juans are found here, though some areas are substantially developed with summer homes (few islanders remain year round). Unfortunately, there are no public facilities on the island. Extensive public tidelands exist, but most are steep and rocky shores to the east and west that are difficult to access. Note that all north-end beach areas within a half-mile of the marina are private.

For the more determined visitor, Blakely's west and southeast shores provide some of the better opportunities for a stroll on a remote beach. Access by kayak may be most practical. The nearest put-in is at Spencer Spit on Lopez Island. Trailered boats can launch at the Obstruction Pass dock on Orcas Island, or at Hunter Bay on Lopez. Be alert for strong currents and tide rips that commonly occur around Obstruction and Peavine Passes, along the easternmost shore of Blakely, and elsewhere. Especially dangerous conditions occur when the tide is ebbing and the wind is out of the south.

Sunset in the San Juans

BLAKELY ISLAND—
1. Blakely Tidelands

Distance: 0.5 to 2.0 miles (or more)

Time: 1 to 2 hours (or more)

Elevation gain: none

NOTE: CHECK THE TIDE TABLES BEFORE HEADING OUT...

There are no public trails on Blakely Island, so the only interest here is in exploring remote and rarely visited rocky beaches. Nearly the entire east and west coastlines of Blakely Island are public, though most of the uplands are private. An exception is a large block of state land with more than a mile of rocky shore on the easternmost part of the island, due west of Strawberry Island off the coast of Cypress. The downside here is that rugged terrain and possible tide rips make the state-owned area generally inaccessible. Much easier beach access exists along the southeast shore of Blakely Island, north of Armitage Island. Wait for calm conditions and a lower tide, then point your kayak, canoe, or dinghy to the obvious beach north of the imposing rock shore near Armitage (be alert for big wake rolling in from the strait). Walk as far north as terrain and tide allow. Note that the protected cove northwest of Armitage is private. The next cove south is public, meaning the beach area only. The land above the driftwood and vegetation line is private property, so please respect it.

A second beach with potential lies on the west shore of the island north of Thatcher Bay and Bald Bluff. About one mile of public shore extends north of the conspicuous rock bluff (Thatcher Bay is private). Like the southeast shore, beaches on the west tend to be a mix of gravel, rubble, and boulders with intermittent headlands. Beaches can be very narrow and impassable at higher tides, although the west side of Blakely is generally more protected than the east. Other public beaches on Blakely tend to be too developed to be of much interest to outsiders. Beaches on the north end are private. A note of caution: accessing Blakely Island in a small craft is not for beginners, due to potentially dangerous conditions (see above).

A view from Camano Island State Park

Camano Island

Island County

To Native Americans, not so many years ago, Camano Island was known as 'Kal-lut-chin' which suggested a land leading into a bay. And that it is, neatly surrounded by the waters of Port Susan, Saratoga Passage, and Skagit Bay, while the northeastern tip is joined to the mainland by a bridge over a slough at Stanwood. Its lengthy shoreline would imply lots of interesting places to explore, but unfortunately, the vast majority of it has been seriously privatized by development. If not for an excellent state park on the west side, Camano Island would have little to offer in the way of trails and walkable beaches for the roving visitor. That seems odd for Island County, considering the many opportunities on neighboring Whidbey Island for the public to enjoy the island life. Camano is an attractive, modest-sized island, but is sadly devoid of hiking opportunities. The exception, as noted, is Camano Island State Park where three short hikes are described.

Despite the skimpy picking's, the future looks a little brighter. Adopted county plans call for several new parks, trails, and beach access areas around the island, including a significant natural area at English Boom on the north end, and the new Cama Beach State Park currently in development next to the existing state park. Adding these and other improvements around the island will provide much needed amenities for residents and visitors alike. Incidentally, traffic can be crazy on Camano Island, so try to avoid the usual commute hours when you visit.

CAMANO ISLAND—
2. The Loop Trail
Distance: 1.9 miles

Time: 1 hour

Elevation gain: minimal

The Loop Trail around Camano Island State Park isn't long, but it does offer an opportunity for a mild workout while enjoying some excellent views and quiet rambling through patches of old-growth forest. Other loops are feasible as well, perhaps taking in the beach in one direction and returning by way of The Loop Trail. Maps are conveniently located at many trail junctions to aid in navigating the park's somewhat complex trail system (new sections constructed in 2001 or later may or may not be displayed).

From Stanwood, 5 miles west of I-5, continue west on SR 532 and follow the signs to Camano Island State Park (curve left, then keep right on Elger Bay Road, right at Mountain View Road, and left on Lowell Point Road). Enter the park and stay left at a curve, parking just ahead at the first small turn-out on the right (*see map, p. 58*). There are several logical places to begin the walk, but the start described here offers a bit of a buffer from the camping and picnicking crowds on summer weekends. Walk down the steps, turn right, and then left at a four-way junction to find the top of the bluff close by. Follow the bluff trail a few yards to an excellent viewpoint with

Lowell Point, from The Loop Trail

a bench. The Olympics rise above Whidbey Island; Mount Rainier is visible to the far left.

Continue about 0.5 mile then turn left and left again to reach the campground road (a right at either of these last two junctions will take you past a group campsite to another path leading steeply down to the beach). At the campground road head right, then look for the Loop Trail sign on the right just around a road bend. Pass the amphitheater, cross a paved road, then angle left to cross the road leading to Point Lowell. Here the path runs along the left side of the road, sometimes on the road shoulder to a bend at the bluff. Walk toward the wood fence for another good view, about 0.9 mile from the start. Continue left along the bluff, winding through forest with gentle ups and downs past a few large Douglas firs over the next 0.6 mile. At a junction with a wide path one can turn right for a slightly shorter finish, though staying left is more interesting. Go left, cross a road, then take the new trail on the right about 0.4 mile to where a quick right leads up to the trailhead. (If turning right onto the wide path noted earlier, walk 0.4 mile to turn left, cross the road, then head left and left again to complete the loop).

CAMANO ISLAND—
3. Saratoga Beach & Point Lowell

Distance: 0.5 to 4.6 miles round trip

Time: 1 to 3 hours

Elevation gain: none

NOTE: CHECK THE TIDE TABLES BEFORE HEADING OUT...

The best public beach walk on Camano Island is along 1.3 miles of Saratoga Passage at Camano Island State Park, plus another mile to Cama Beach State Park (in development, mid-2001). Most of the shore is coarse gravel, with sandy areas on the upper beach. An accretion beach has formed at Point Lowell near the south boundary of the park as a result of many years of deposition of these eroded sediments. This material is transported in small amounts by wind, waves and currents day after day, year after year. To visualize the process in simple terms, imagine every wave stirring and scouring the sediments, and every calm moment allowing some or all of these sediments to settle out. If more material settles than stirs, we find accretion. If more is stirred up or washed away than is settled, the shore will erode. All of this while the water is moving up and down the shore, ever changing with the weather and tides.

Begin either at Point Lowell or North Beach (see Hike 2 for directions). If starting at the latter, the short path to the beach is near

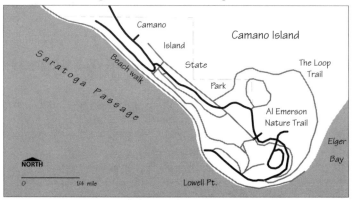

the information kiosk. Wander northward (right) below bluffs toward Cama Beach, or south (left) to Point Lowell. If walking south, pass a trail leading back up to the picnic area just before the bluff begins to rise. From here it is 0.5 mile to the point. Whidbey Island and the Olympic Mountains dominate the view. Continue past picnic tables or head left at the boat ramp to the Marsh Trail along the base of the bluff past a remnant backwater marsh (spring birding potential). The Marsh Trail ends at a junction next to the road where you can either head back out to the beach for the return, or trudge up the hill to follow one of the upper trails back to the start. If heading up the hill, stay left, climb steps and switchbacks for 100 yards, then stay right to find the campground road (see Hike 2 for more).

Camano Island—
4. Al Emerson Nature Trail

Distance: 0.5-mile loop
Time: 1/2 hour
Elevation gain: minimal

Camano Island State Park is also home to the Al Emerson Nature Trail, an interesting interpretive trail in an old-growth forest. A well-written brochure describes many of the trees and shrubs you will encounter along the 0.5-mile loop. Pick one up at the trailhead and return it at the end of your hike. Although the trail needs no description here, of particular interest are several large Douglas fir trees, possibly 600 years old, and an unusually large Pacific yew tree. Natural floral diversity makes this a great place for young naturalists to learn many of the more common species found in northwest Washington forests.

Head up the park entrance road, stay left at the curve, and find a well-signed trailhead on the left 0.5 mile ahead. Begin the loop on the left. The trail is named for Al Emerson, who worked at the park for many years and appreciated its unique qualities as much as anyone. This light stroll can be easily added to The Loop Trail (Hike 2) by heading back up the main road 0.1 mile from the campground.

Clark Island

San Juan County

One of two skinny, remote islands east of Orcas and west across Rosario Strait from Lummi Island, uninhabited Clark Island offers a good view across the strait to Lummi Island and beyond. (Smaller Barnes Island to the west is entirely private though minimally developed; its tidelands are public.) Shores are rugged sandstone to the north and south, with modest gravel beaches east and west separated by a narrow neck of land—it's barely a stone's throw from one beach to the other.

Primitive campsites are available on Clark, and mooring buoys exist offshore of both beaches though they are somewhat exposed to the whims of weather and water. Smaller craft can haul out easily on either

Madrona trees on Clark Island

beach, though there is no easy approach. Experienced kayakers often launch from North Beach on Orcas Island, five miles away, or Lummi Island, which is closer but requires a committing 2.5-mile crossing of the strait and shipping channel—no place for novice boaters. Trailered boats generally launch from Bellingham, Anacortes, or from public launches within the San Juans. The Sisters lie offshore Clark's south end; these large treeless rocks are protected as part of the National Wildlife Refuge (two 200-yard rule applies).

CLARK ISLAND—
5. Clark Island Marine State Park

Distance: 0.5 mile
Time: 1 hour
Elevation gain: minimal

To protect wildlife, Washington State Parks now manages Clark Island as an essentially trailless island. That's good for the birds and marine mammals, but a little unsettling for those who have enjoyed the short scenic hike around the island's south end for years. The small campground remains, however, sandwiched on the narrow neck of land between opposing beaches. Connected by a short path through the campground, the sand and gravel beaches offer a fine short saunter, but the closure of the bluff trail at the south end severely constrains enjoyment of an otherwise lovely, uncrowded island park. The trail closure might encourage some to scramble along the rocky shores at the south end, perhaps as disruptive to wildlife as was the old path above the bluff. A better solution might have been (and still could be) to relocate portions of the southerly path away from the bluff and around the most sensitive areas, or at least make the closure seasonal as is done in many other locations. Despite this minor grumbling, we all want our wildlife protected. For now, enjoy Clark Island for its intermittent solitude, placid camping, seabird watching, and wide views from Georgia Strait to the North Cascades.

Cypress Island

Skagit County

Cypress Island, imprecisely named for its Rocky Mountain juniper trees by Captain Vancouver in 1792, represents the largest state-owned protected area in the islands of northwest Washington. The lands are managed by the Washington Department of Natural Resources (DNR). With recent acquisitions, almost 3,900 acres of the island's 5,500 acres are included in the Cypress Island Natural Resource Conservation Area. Another 1,000-plus acres are designated Natural Area Preserve, providing a high level of protection for sensitive plant and animal communities. Less than 600 acres are privately owned. Protected areas include unique forest, grassland, wetlands, and several small lakes, as well as nesting habitat for sensitive bird species and other wildlife. The island also hosts two campgrounds, more than 25 miles of trails (hiker-only), interpretive facilities, and mooring buoys to facilitate boat access. There are only a few permanent residents. All access is by private boat only.

Over the past several thousand years, Cypress was used by Native Americans for summer hunting and fishing activities. The use subsided, not surprisingly, after the first non-native settler arrived in 1866. Cypress Island soon attracted a wide range of "foreigners" with their own ambitions: trappers, farmers, loggers, miners, fishers, boatbuilders, ice cream makers, and later a health resort and Boy Scout camp.

In the 1960s, Cypress Island Development Corporation acquired much of the island, and plans were made in the 1970s for massive residential development and a major conference center. The public objected and following a great deal of effort on the part of Friends of Cypress Island, Cypress Island Natural History Association, and others, the DNR successfully negotiated the purchase of lands from the developer in 1987. The area was immediately designated one of the state's first Natural Resource Conservation Areas. Although Cypress is part of the San Juan archipelago, this conspicuous and mountainous island is within Skagit County, three miles northwest of Anacortes.

The 5,500-acre island has much to offer in the way of great views,

Lummi Island from the Cypress airstrip

pleasant forest, rugged coastline, quiet beaches, and hidden lakes, all of which are well linked by trails to a number of access points. The Eagle Cliff Trail on the north tip of Cypress is the most popular destination, while many other areas receive relatively few visitors, offering some of the better opportunities for solitude in the islands. Hiking on Cypress is always a charm, but for one notable downside. The trail builders relied excessively on old logging roads to connect the dots, which means a lot of walking through less interesting disturbed areas, with hardly a view and rarely a stick of old growth. Where new trails were built, they are generally well constructed—the stone steps above Cypress Head, for example (see Hike 9). Yet with only a few deviations, some trails could have easily incorporated outstanding views from rocky points and meadowy ridges. Hopefully, the DNR will entertain a few minor reroutes away from old road sections and a handful of short spurs to scenic viewpoints, while still maintaining highly sensitive areas and unique ecological characteristics that clearly deserve protection.

Hand-launched craft often put in next to the Guemes Island Ferry dock in Anacortes, or at Washington Park just southwest of the San Juan Island Ferry terminal (see Hikes 19 and 13 for directions). Some paddlers combine a stop at Strawberry Island with a visit to Cypress. There are no public docks, though mooring buoys exist off Pelican Beach (unprotected) and Cypress Head (partially protected). Campsites exist at these locations, as well as at Strawberry. For paddlers, significant currents, tide rips, and open channel crossings make any approach a serious one, even in fair weather. As with access to all other islands, novice paddlers should not attempt these crossings without an experienced paddler along who can help assure the preparedness and safety of the group.

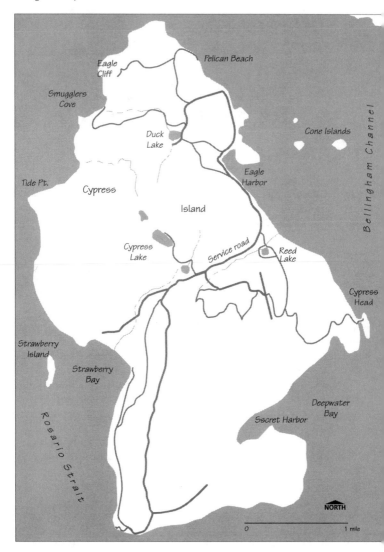

CYPRESS ISLAND—
6. Eagle Cliff
Distance: 2.6 miles (or more) round trip

Time: 2 to 3 hours

Elevation gain: 800 feet

NOTE: TRAIL IS CLOSED FEBRUARY THROUGH MID-JULY

One of the more dramatic rock walls in the San Juan archipelago is Eagle Cliff, rising above the north tip of Cypress Island. The namesake eagles are a common sight here, but they have become a fairly common sight throughout the islands in recent years, having rebounded somewhat from their previous demise. In fact, the San Juans host one of the highest year-round concentrations of eagles in the continental U.S. Nevertheless, bald eagle populations are still well below historic numbers, but the fact that these majestic soaring

Blakely Island from Eagle Cliff

creatures are so large and conspicuous against the sky make them easy to recognize. Thus they may seem more common than they really are. When you do see them, savor the sight and their delicate vocalizations, for America's icon of freedom, justice, and wildness is still a protected species under the Endangered Species Act.

The 1.3-mile hike to the top of Eagle Cliff is a local favorite, that is, when the trail is open. To protect the eagles, falcons, and other wildlife in the area, the trail is closed to the public from February 1st to July 15th each year. When it is open, the cliff trail is well connected to the island's extensive trail system and can be accessed from several points, with the shortest and most popular route from the Pelican Beach DNR campground on the northeast shore. Eagle Harbor offers convenient access as well, but is almost a mile farther (see Hike 8). A less traveled route from a small bay on Cypress' northwest shore is also quite feasible. There are small beaches but no docks at all three locations.

From Pelican Beach, follow the short boardwalk and stairs past an impressive monument to composting toilets. Then head rightward on a path to several large interpretive signs that help set the mood for exploring (similar signs elsewhere on the island, like those at Eagle Harbor, provide an excellent introduction to the island's natural and cultural history). Stay on the path, really an old road bed, through once-cut forest to a signed junction at 0.3 mile (straight goes to Duck Lake, Hike 7). Turn right for the 1.0-mile finish to the top of Eagle Cliff. This trail climbs gradually, levels out, then steepens again as it leaves the dense forest, passing several good viewpoints the last 0.2-mile to the summit. The views are immense: Orcas Island to the northwest across Rosario Strait, Lummi Island to the north, Sinclair and Vendovi Islands below to the northeast, with Mount Baker beyond, the Chuckanut mainland and Blanchard Mountain to the east, Bellingham Channel and Guemes Island to the southeast, sprawling Cypress Island to the south, and Blakely Island and the Olympic Mountains to the southwest.

CYPRESS ISLAND—
7. Duck Lake & Eagle Harbor

Distance: 1.5 to 3.1 miles round trip

Time: 2 to 3 hours

Elevation gain: 600 to 1,200 feet

As noted earlier, Cypress Island trails lead to many destinations, from stunning overlooks and loungable beaches, to quiet coves and rocky meadows. You can experience a good bit of the island's wildness by way of a 3.1-mile loop from Pelican Beach to Duck Lake, Eagle Harbor and back to Pelican (or shorten the round-trip hike to Duck Lake to 1.5 miles by starting at Eagle Harbor). If time—and legs—allow, add a side trip to Eagle Cliff (Hike 6) or Reed Lake (Hike 8) and beyond. Interpretive signs at Pelican and Eagle Harbor provide an added educational perk.

The popular trailhead and campground at Pelican Beach lie on the northeast shore of the island (*map, p. 64*). Hand-launchers can land on the gravel beach near the conspicuous outhouse, while others can tie to mooring buoys offshore. The path heads up a few steps, angles right past signs, then turns southwest on a gradual rise along an old logging road. Pass the spur to Eagle Cliff in 0.3 mile, reaching another junction with a service road 0.2 mile farther. Left drops a mile to Eagle Harbor, but turn right, then right again in 0.2 mile. Duck Lake is just ahead, past a collapsing old cabin. The old road skirts the marshy lake—good bird-watching potential in spring—and descends 1.2 miles to Smugglers Cove south of Eagle Cliff.

Maybe skip the descent and retrace your steps to the last junction and head right to the southeast shore of the lake. The old road swings right at a junction where a signed path on the left leads to Eagle Harbor. Follow this to another road junction, stay on the narrower path and gradually descend to the service road at Eagle Harbor, 1.6 miles from the start. A left here rounds the harbor and climbs a mile to the first Eagle Harbor junction noted above; right leads a short distance to several excellent interpretive signs describing the island history and geology, and continues a mile (mostly uphill) to Reed Lake. The scenic harbor makes a good lunch stop.

CYPRESS ISLAND—
8. Reed Lake & Cypress Lake

Distance: 2.7 to 5.5 miles (or more) round trip

Time: 2 to 4 hours

Elevation gain: 600 to 1,200 feet

From Cypress Island's Eagle Harbor, a number of dayhikes are possible, including Duck Lake and Eagle Cliff (see Hike 6), and the moderately steep but straightforward hike to Reed and Cypress Lakes. A longer loop trek to Bradberry Lake and the abandoned airstrip is a reasonable option as well. Most of the hike is along boring old roads, so save your down time for the lakes and Eagle Harbor itself, the principal harbor on the north half of the island. As described in the introduction, access for paddlers requires significant open water crossings, easy for experienced kayakers, but much more risky for novices due to strong currents, tide rips, and the everpresent threats of wind and waves.

Find the road above the harbor's scenic beach and head left into the woods (*map, p. 64*). Several exceptionally informative interpretive signs add some interest to the hike ahead. In 0.3 mile continue straight ahead on the main service road (right goes to Duck Lake, left drops back down to the harbor). In 0.7 mile more, reach the Reed Lake junction. If doing the longer Bradberry Lake loop, save Reed for later; otherwise turn left here, pass a DNR service area and find the lake loop on the right just ahead. Round the marshy constructed lake (swimming is allowed), and go left at the road to return to the first Reed Lake junction. Follow the road again left for about 0.7 mile to the Bradberry/airstrip junction and continue straight another 0.1 mile to the Cypress Lake junction. (From here, ambitious hikers can follow the road all the way to its end near Reef Point, about 2.4 miles distant, and return via the Reef Point and Strawberry Bay Trails, there and back again adding another 6.0 miles or more to the trip. These trails can also be accessed from Strawberry Bay.)

It may be enough for most mortals to turn right on the Cypress Lake Trail. Walk about 0.5 mile to a junction just beyond a small

"Cypress" tree (Rocky Mountain juniper) on Cypress Lake

stream crossing and turn right (straight works too, but right is more scenic). The old road narrows to a path that emerges just above the lake. A short descent leads to an open area with a place to sit and soak up the rays. Though it may be tempting, there's no swimming here since Cypress Lake supplies water to residents at Strawberry Bay. A rough boot track continues around the lake but the going is cumbersome and the views get no better.

Either retrace your steps for the return (5.5 miles round trip), or turn right (southeast) at the junction preceding the Cypress Lake Trail to hike the longer loop to Bradberry Lake and the airstrip (see Hike 9). Taking in both lake and airstrip adds about 2.5 miles to the return, or 1.5 miles if you skip Bradberry. If approaching Reed Lake from Cypress Head, continue north (straight) from the airstrip/Reed Lake junction; go 0.6 mile, then left to loop around that lake.

CYPRESS ISLAND—
9. Cypress Head & Bradberry Lake

Distance: 4.6 to 9.2 miles round trip
Time: 3 to 6 hours
Elevation gain: 800 feet

Cypress Head, the easternmost tip of Cypress Island, is also one of the more scenic spots around the island. A small boaters campground here attracts many weekend travelers in summer, though you might have the place to yourself midweek or in the off-season. A 0.3-mile loop around the rocky forested headland offers great views of Bellingham Channel, surrounding islands, as well as the narrow tombolo and back-to-back coves that separate Cypress Head from the rest of Cypress Island. The tombolo, or connecting sand and gravel beach, also serves as a trailhead for Bradberry, Reed, and Cypress Lakes, and an abandoned airstrip—an anomolous, shaved plain with a view, perched high above the channel.

To reach the trailhead, aim for Cypress Head, the conspicuous "islet" on the east shore connected to the rest of the island by a low beach. Currents in Bellingham Channel, between Cypress and Guemes, can be very strong, with tide rips forming close to shore. Paddlers should only round the head at or near slack current times. Land at either the north or south beach. There is no dock, but there are mooring buoys in the north cove. The path around Cypress Head is easy to find, leading south from the picnic tables and campsites on either side. The northeast side is a good place to watch the tide rips roiling a hundred feet offshore.

For the stiff 2.2-mile hike up to Bradberry Lake, find the trail marker at the west end of the tombolo and head up, steeply at first, soon meeting an old road bed. Stay on the beaten track and in 0.3 mile watch for a signpost pointing right at a road junction. Take a quick look back—it's easy to make a wrong turn here on the way back. The well marked trail crosses three roads (leading through private lands) over the next 0.2 mile, and reaches a junction at 1.5 mile. Turn left for Bradberry Lake, or continue straight for a longer loop taking in Reed and Cypress Lakes. For the latter, hike 0.6 mile to the next Reed Lake junction (see Hike 8 for the continuation to Cypress Lake).

From the Bradberry Lake junction, head left to find the airstrip in 0.3 mile. There are good views from both ends of the strip that are worth the extra walking (to the north see the Cone Islands, Sinclair, Lummi, and Eliza Islands, and Bellingham beyond; from the south the view spans from Mount Baker to Mount Rainier, plus Guemes and Samish Islands, Anacortes, and Mount Erie). From the airstrip signpost, walk right 100 yards, then left 100 yards and watch for another signpost well to the left just before the road ahead begins to curve right. It's a steep 0.3 mile more to reach this skinny lake stopped up by a small earthen dam. A bog and large meadow nearby are rich with wildflowers in spring. Swimming is allowed but shallow water and a mucky bottom may not be too appealing for some of us. This round-trip hike to Bradberry, including the view from the north end of the airstrip, is 4.6 miles. If continuing on to Cypress Lake, follow the path (old road bed) north and west another 1.1 miles to the well-used road leading 0.5 mile back up and east to the airstrip (right). Instead go left 0.3 mile, then left again 0.1 mile to the Cypress Lake junction, then right 0.5 mile to the lake.

Hauled out at Cypress Head

Paddling off Decatur's White Cliff Beach

Decatur Island

San Juan County

Other than a county dock, a cross-island road, and a few miles of
public tidelands, Decatur Island, east of Lopez, is essentially
private and of little interest to hikers—unless, of course, you live
there. Decatur is also one of the larger non-ferry islands so you are
on your own getting there. Kayakers can explore the entire coastline in settled weather, but beware of tide rips and dangerous conditions between Thatcher Pass north of James Island and Rosario
Strait, especially when the tide is ebbing and the wind is from the
south. Extensive tidelands along Thatcher Pass are steep and rocky,
while only limited areas of public beach exist on the west shore. The
exposed southeast shore, described below, offers the best opportunity for a beach ramble.

DECATUR ISLAND—
10. White Cliff Beach

Distance: 1 mile (or more)

Time: 1 hour

Elevation gain: none

NOTE: CHECK THE TIDE TABLES BEFORE HEADING OUT...

The two-mile-long public beach on Decatur Island's southeast shore faces the open water of Rosario Strait and can, therefore, be exposed to wind and waves. In stable weather and low to moderate tides, rowers and paddlers can aim for the sandy beach at the south end of the rising bluff (most of the low beach farther south is private). To the north, the beach is more gravelly, becoming coarse and narrow with scattered boulders. The public tideland extends all the way to Decatur Head, across from James Island. The walk is wild and remote, with the exception of a single home close to shore near the midway point. White Cliff is a 100-foot-high eroding bluff composed of light-colored sediments.

Cypress Island rises above James Island to the northeast of White Cliff Beach; Fidalgo, Burrows, and Allan Islands lie to the east; Fidalgo Island's Mount Erie and Whidbey Island are to the southeast; and Lopez Island's Sperry Peninsula sits to the south. One could feasibly reach the north end of the beach from the county dock by walking county roads south and east. Note that the north-facing beach adjacent to, and west of, Decatur Head is private. Paddlers might also consider a brief stop on a small south-facing beach at Decatur's south end. A short path leads up the knob on the left to another viewpoint.

Doe Island

San Juan County

Just six scenic acres in size, Doe Island is around the corner from the Doe Bay Resort on southeast Orcas Island. Campsites, an outhouse and trails are provided. Beaches for landing small boats are scarce, especially at very high and very low tides. The best landing is either at a dock and float on the north side (more protected), or at the small gravel beach near the southeast point. A small rocky beach in the middle of the south shore is also a possibility. The shortest approach for boaters may be from the county's Obstruction Pass boat ramp a few miles to the southwest, though most visitors simply include a stop at Doe as part of a bigger cruise. Guided kayak trips from Doe Bay provide another means of accessing the island.

South shore, Doe Island

DOE ISLAND—
11. Doe Island Marine State Park

Distance: 0.5-mile loop

Time: 1 hour

Elevation gain: minimal

Close to the southeast shore of Orcas Island, a number of homes in the area make little Doe Island seem fairly civilized. Yet the south shore is about as wild and scenic as any marine state park in the San Juans. Several campsites along this shore are perched above a rocky bluff overlooking the uninhabited parts of Cypress and Blakely Islands which loom in the dusk as great dark masses with almost no sign of humanity. Only the blinking navigation lights remind you that civilization hasn't left. In the daylight hours, find a lovely forest, storm-swept rocky shores, and about 0.5 mile of good trails circling and crossing the island.

The trails really require no description. Begin anywhere and turn randomly at junctions. There are more or less two loops, one east and one west. The forest and coast are pretty enough that one can easily wander them all in both directions, and then some. At lower tides, one can also scramble along the rocky southern and eastern shores without much difficulty. Otherwise, stay on the trails to avoid scrunching the vegetation.

Fidalgo Island

Skagit County

It's easy not to notice that Fidalgo is an island. On the drive to Anacortes on SR 20 from I-5, the highway traverses a very large bridge over the Swinomish Slough, the narrow waterway that separates Fidalgo Island from the mainland. And though Fidalgo is much smaller than Orcas or San Juan Islands, it feels bigger than it is, perhaps because there is so much here: a small, attractive waterfront city (Skagit's second largest), the San Juan Islands Ferry terminal, the Swinomish Indian Nation, a lovely coastline, scenic beaches, rocky headlands, several thousand acres of community-owned forest, several lakes, an assortment of parks and trails, and the crowning summit of Mount Erie (see Hike 16).

Around the turn of the century, Fidalgo was thought to have potential as a west coast railroad terminus for Jim Hill's Great Northern Railroad. But the tracks leaned south to Seattle instead. Still another plot envisioned an over-the-water rail link to Whidbey Island (and another to Port Townsend), but that idea fell just as flat. In the meantime, investors, speculators and residents had discovered enough about Fidalgo's remarkable natural assets to begin to build a community that would persist well into the future. Oil refineries and tourism are key industries, with the latter having grown to millions of people each year as many travelers either head for the San Juan Islands, or make the trip across Deception Pass to Whidbey Island and beyond.

Anacortes from Cap Sante

FIDALGO ISLAND—
12. Cap Sante Overlook

Distance: 0.8 mile round trip

Time: 1 hour

Elevation gain: 200 feet

Many visitors to Anacortes probably don't see much more of this interesting city than the mundane business strip leading to the San Juan Islands Ferry terminal. But get off the busy ferry route and you will find more to appreciate about the place, including the excellent overlook at Cap Sante Park. While it's possible to drive there, a rough and steep trail provides a worthwhile alternative for hikers. From Commercial Avenue, the main drag through Anacortes, turn right (east) on Fourth Street, then right again in a few blocks at a small Rotary Park sign just before Fourth Street heads up the hill (which is the auto route to the overlook). After two blocks angle left on a gravel road to find a small trailhead parking area.

Walk the paved path a few yards to a junction where one can wander to the right around the boat harbor for some extra rambling. To reach the overlook, keep going 100 yards to a beach access (and more rambling at lower tides). The paved path continues a short distance to a picnic shelter, but turn left up the stairs to an unpaved path. Follow this right, staying left at the next two junctions. A short steep section and light rock scrambling (can be slick when wet) lead to scenic, open ground above. Follow path and bare rock to the highest point and a near-360-degree view. This is a good place to linger since most of the car-people tend to stay below. Enjoy a fine view of Anacortes, Mount Erie, March Point, Guemes Island, Mount Baker, and the North Cascades. Look toward the parking area to find a beaten track leading down to the right. There is more exploring beyond, but drop-offs and/or wet rock suggest a measure of caution. Retrace the route for the return.

FIDALGO ISLAND—
13. Fidalgo Head

Distance: 1.7 to 3.3 miles round trip
Time: 1 to 2 hours
Elevation gain: 300 to 600 feet

For an easy sampling of what Skagit County's Fidalgo Island has to offer, try the 1.7-mile (or longer) hike around Fidalgo Head at Washington Park, west of Anacortes. Cool forest, rocky shores, island views, and rosy sunsets await, regardless of the season. If going for the latter, at least take a flashlight—the woods are very dark at dusk, and you could turn and ankle on occasional rough spots on the trail if you can't see past your knees.

To reach the trail, drive SR 20 into downtown Anacortes and head for the San Juan Islands Ferry terminal about three miles west of Commercial Avenue. The way is well signed. As you approach the turn for the ferry, move to the left lane and proceed straight onto Sunset Ave. About 0.8 mile farther, enter the park and turn right at either the "Picnic Area" or "Beach Area" sign. Park, then head leftward (west) along the shore a short distance to find the trail sign in bushes next to the beach. The path is in generally good shape with a few roots and rocks. Vegetation crowds the way in several places, so rainpants are useful on cool, wet days. Occasional sidetrails can confuse the route, but the main track is fairly obvious most of the way, and marked by numerous signs.

*Green Point
at Fidalgo Head*

The Fidalgo Head Loop is easy and scenic from the start, with a lush understory of salal up to seven feet high, pleasant Douglas fir forest, and good views of Cypress Island to the north. In less than 0.2 mile, the path turns left to cross a road (a spur here leads 0.3 mile to Green Point for an optional side trip, though one more easily visited by car or bike). Reach a signed trail junction at 0.4 mile and continue straight across to begin a gradual climb to another road crossing. Keep rising, pass a small clearing with a view amid scattered Rocky Mountain juniper trees, then another signed junction for Juniper Point—a mandatory side trip. Saunter right 100 yards to a bench with an exceptional view of Burrows Island, the San Juans,

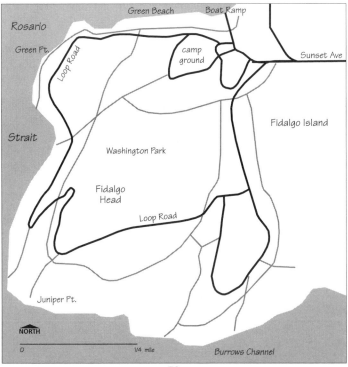

and in the distance, Juan de Fuca Strait between Burrows and Lopez Islands.

Head back to the loop trail, wander past the next sign, stay left at a dip, then climb again for more good views. Just over a mile from the start, a quarter-mile spur (signed) heads right to Burrows Channel, dropping about 200 feet en route to a tiny, solitary cove—another optional side trip. Now it's decision time: Plan A is to skip the spur and follow the main loop to where it crosses the road again with about 0.4 mile to go, all of it downhill. Stay right at the next junction then left on a paved road. Pick up the trail again on the right, and in a few yards, head left to meet the park access road adjacent to the "Beach Area" parking sign. Including Juniper Point, this loop is 1.7 miles long, or 2.8 miles with side trips to Green Point and Burrows Channel.

The longer, more scenic, and slightly complex Plan B is to head down the Burrows Channel spur, turning right at the first junction and left at the next (right drops to the water's edge), then up and over a low rock step into meadow with scattered trees. Stay right, the trail descends a bit, then levels out. There are several paths in the area, so the basic idea is to continue to where a spur drops 100 yards to a rocky perch near the water. Two paths head more steeply uphill from here (the left is easier). Enjoy the excellent view of Burrows Island, and hike up and right below the top of the knoll (the road is just above) then follow a more level path 0.1 mile farther to a monument (to pioneer Havekost). In about 0.1 mile more, stay left. In another 0.1 mile, stay right; walk between hedge-like bushes, then stay left, walking another 0.1 mile and passing through two interesting "tunnels" of vegetation. Go right again, and in 0.2 mile head more or less straight at a four-way junction. Reach the last junction in 0.1 mile, hang a left, and emerge from the woods across from the parking area. The maze of trails can be confusing, but the route described is direct, scenic, and generally downhill. If you find yourself disoriented, or if mud or brush make the going unpleasant, generally head left to find the paved road and simply follow it down to the parking area. Plan B adds about 0.5 mile to the hike.

FIDALGO ISLAND—
14. Little Cranberry Lake

Distance: 3.4– to 4.3–mile loops (or more)

Time: 2 to 3 hours (or more)

Elevation gain: minimal

For a pleasant walk around a small lake and nearby wetlands, plus a chance to see a beaver slapping its tail against the water, try the loop hike around Little Cranberry Lake on Fidalgo Island west of Anacortes. "Little" helps distinguish this area from the much larger Cranberry Lake at Deception Pass State Park. The lake and several beaver ponds are completely surrounded by the Anacortes Community Forest Lands and interconnected by an extensive multi-use trail system that offers almost endless possibilities for shorter and longer hikes. The route suggested below takes in several trails that are designated hiker–only, and short sections that are open to bikes and/or motorcycles, though you are unlikely to encounter many of the latter. Detailed maps of the community forest lands are available for purchase at city hall, bookstores, and bike and outdoor shops in Anacortes—and well worth the investment.

Little Cranberry Lake

You can access the Little Cranberry Lake area from many locations, but the description here begins at a small parking area next to A Avenue and just south of 37th Street. If heading into Anacortes from SR 20 turn left on 32nd Street, then left again on D Avenue which soon jogs right to become 37th, then jogs left at A Avenue. (A larger parking area at the lake can be reached from SR 20 on the way to the San Juan Islands ferry terminal. Turn south on Georgia Avenue then right in three blocks on a gravel road that leads to the lake—a good place to launch a canoe.) Pass the gate and walk the road 0.1 mile to a junction; turn right, then stay left just ahead on Trail 108. Take the next right, soon crossing a small bridge at a wetland, then go left, now on a hiker-only path. Amble past Big Beaver Pond to the next junction and head left. A few yards beyond, descend to Little Cranberry Lake nearby, 0.9 mile from the start.

Walk right along the shore (some rough spots). Near the north end, the trail passes below a cliff where several large boulders provide a great perch for a little nature observation. Just ahead, a short spur climbs to an old mine shaft. Staying left, continue around a skinny northeastern arm of the lake before reaching a small dam and parking area at the lake's outlet. From here, simply follow the paths rimming the west side of the lake by staying left at junctions, but always on a well trodden path. Pass a big rock slab (another good resting spot), then just after crossing a bridge near the southwest corner of the lake, watch for the next fork and go left, dropping slightly. This section has a few muddy spots in the wet season and plenty of roots and rocks to stumble over, but it's passable. At the next bridge, you will have completed the 1.6-mile loop around Little Cranberry. Go late in the day and you may just see (or hear) a beaver nosing around the south end of the lake.

From this point, either retrace your earlier steps back to the start, or, to walk the loop around Big Beaver Pond, stay right (don't cross the bridge), then go left in 0.1 mile. From here, stay left at all junctions (except faint paths that tend to deadend) until you reach a short spur on the left, Trail 125, which leads fifty yards to a bridge and tiny island. Continue on the main path 0.1 mile and go left at the next junction. Finally, 0.2 mile farther, stay right this time to return to the gravel road. A Avenue is 0.1 mile to the left.

FIDALGO ISLAND—
15. Heart Lake

Distance: 1.9– to 3.0–mile loops
Time: 1 to 2 hours
Elevation gain: 200 to 400 feet

Though Heart Lake State Park provides only minimal facilities, is well enough known for pleasant fishing and light boating to receive moderate weekend use spring through fall. For some, the lake is a welcome alternative to faster, noisier boating on Campbell Lake a few miles to the south. Unlike Campbell, Heart Lake's shores are essentially undeveloped, plus there is a magnificent patch of old-growth forest on the south shore, with Douglas firs in the range of four to six feet in diameter. You can opt for a short hike in the woods or a loop around the lake, although the latter requires either walking the road briefly (on a very narrow grass shoulder), or taking a longer detour up and down the mountainside—a short connector path nearer the road is sorely needed here. Anacortes Community Forest Lands surround the park on all but the west side.

A good starting point is at the small parking area at the base of the Mount Erie Road, just off Heart Lake Road. From SR 20 at milepost 46.1, turn north on Campbell Lake Road and angle right in 1.5 miles on Heart Lake Road. In 1.4 miles more, take the Mount Erie turnoff on the right (*map, p. 86*). Park near the information kiosk, then walk the gravel drive over to Heart Lake Road to find the trail next to a sign for "Pine Ridge Loop." Walk a few yards, head right, then turn right again in 0.2 mile. The path descends into the old growth, a powerful reminder of what much of our lowland forest once looked like. Enjoy this part of the walk, sometimes close to the shore, then reach a junction nearly a mile from the start. Turn right for the lake loop, or go left 0.1 mile and left again 0.8 more to loop back to the beginning (1.9 miles total).

If continuing around the lake, stay right on a rough path in younger forest, skirt a marsh, and then the lake, before drifting away from the water to reach the next fork 0.6 mile from the last. Head right 0.2 mile, then take several more rights, generally paralleling the lakeshore. At the boat ramp, 2.0 miles from the start, head first left, then cross the road. From this point, the easier route is to walk south (right) along the grassy edge of Heart Lake Road for 0.2 mile to a wide trail with a gate on the left. This gate is beyond a wide turn-out and just around a bend in the road. However, the road narrows for 100 yards, leaving very little room to walk in the grass—and poor visibility for drivers. Do not walk this route if you feel it may be unsafe (see below for a slightly longer option that doesn't require walking along the road). From the gate, ascend through beautiful old-growth forest for 0.1 mile to a giant seven-foot diameter fir tree and make a sharp right. Saunter through more old-growth forest for 0.2 mile and turn right at a big cedar tree for the flat and easy return to the beginning (2.7 miles total).

An alternative to walking along the road is to cross at the boat launch and head up the obvious path, continuing straight ahead at a nearby four-way junction. In 0.2 mile more turn right, ascend 0.2 mile, then go right again (down) to reach the 7-foot fir (mentioned above) in 100 yards. Stay left here, then right for the finish. This longer version of the lake loop is 0.3 mile longer and gains an extra 100 feet of elevation.

The extensive trail system on adjoining state park and community forest lands offers almost unlimited options for additional hiking, though a detailed trail map is essential (available at city hall, bookstores, and bike and outdoor shops).

Campbell Lake and Whidbey Island from Mount Erie

16. Mount Erie & Sugarloaf

Distance: 0.6 to 4.8 miles round trip

Time: 1 to 3 hours

Elevation gain: 250 to 1,000 feet

With a narrow paved road winding up to the scenic summit of Fidalgo Island, few will bother hiking up the mountain. Nevertheless, there is a certain satisfaction that goes along with doing Mount Erie "the hard way," even if it isn't all that difficult, at least by North Cascades standards. The hike itself is nondescript, but the views from the top, of course, are spectacular. With all the dramatic terrain around the upper several hundred feet of Mount Erie, it seems odd that the trail was not routed to take advantage of interesting rock formations and more good views. Another downside is that there is no alternative route for the descent, other than the road.

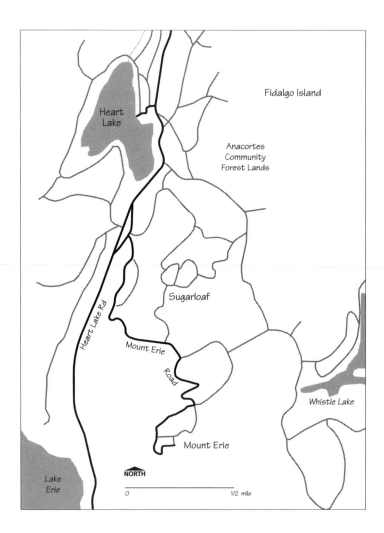

The area really deserves an around-the-mountain loop, or at least an optional descent route that honors the unique qualities of this beautiful place.

Grumbling aside, the hike up Erie can begin either at the trailhead at the base of the Mount Erie Road (2.4 miles one–way), or at an intermediate trailhead midway up (1.1 mile). The former is more enjoyable as it climbs up and over Sugarloaf, which by itself makes a good short hike to a nice viewpoint. However, the route loses and regains an extra 250 feet of elevation on the way to Erie. To reach the lower trailhead from SR 20, turn west on Campbell Lake Road at milepost 46.1 and angle right in 1.5 miles on Heart Lake Road. The Mount Erie turnoff is 1.4 miles ahead on the right.

Begin at the trail information sign and walk an easy 0.2 mile to a junction at a giant cedar tree. Turn right and begin climbing steeply on a good path that is, amazingly, open to motorized use. At 0.3 mile, stay right on Trail 215 from which motorbikes are banned, and follow this trail about 0.4 mile to a good viewpoint on the right. Lopez Island and Juan de Fuca Strait are to the left, Burrows Island and Fidalgo Head are straight ahead, with Cypress Island to the right and Orcas behind it. Note the glacial grooves in the rock. Reach another junction just ahead and head right briefly (the trail descends slightly) to the next junction. Here, a right drops 0.2 mile to the Mount Erie Road, making this a much easier access to Sugarloaf (but not much of a hike). Instead, go left to an opening with a view, then back into the woods briefly, ignoring a rough spur on the right.

Take the next right at a T junction (Trail 238, remember this turn) and quickly reach an open rocky meadow near the summit of Sugarloaf, just over a mile from the trailhead. Allan, Burrows, and Lopez Islands are now to the right, and Lake Erie is below, with the Olympic Mountains and Whidbey Island visible beyond the forested side of Mount Erie nearby. Left is Similk Bay and Kiket, Skagit, Hope, and Goat Islands.

For the continuation to Mount Erie, retrace your steps to the earlier junction and descend through rock gardens 0.2 mile to the Mount Erie Road (the trail is braided—it forks and rejoins). Cautiously walk the road left 0.1 mile to a sign for the summit trail on the left (parking here for 2 or 3 cars). Follow this an easy 0.2 mile to a junction with a trail leading to Whistle Lake (drops nearly 400 feet in 0.6 mile), but continue straight ahead on generally rough trail for 0.5 mile, passing a braided section, to meet the road again at a hairpin turn. Two left turns are feasible immediately before the road. They rejoin above, though the second is easier.

Near the summit, more braided paths confuse the route coming down, so keep track of the turns. From the top, one can find the route down immediately across the road from a microwave tower in the right corner of a small parking area. Walk a few yards to see the sign for Trail 216. Wander the summit area for views in several directions—extra caution is advised for younger kids since some of the paths, used by rock climbers, lead right over the brink. Interpretive signs describe the views. The easiest descent is to follow the road (1.7 miles), or some combination of road and trail. If walking the road, stay totally alert for cars on blind corners. The entire hike to the top including Sugarloaf is about 2.4 miles.

FIDALGO ISLAND—
17. Sharpe Marsh & Bluff

Distance: 1.0 mile

Time: 1 hour

Elevation gain: 100 feet

What appears to be a simple little park in the country turns out to offer much more than a pastoral picnic in the grass. The path at Skagit County's Sharpe Park leads past a seemingly primeval swamp on the way to a great overlook of the islands and the sea off the west coast of Fidalgo Island—a good bird-watching destination as well. The trail is in generally good condition, though with minimal improvements, it could be made barrier-free at least to the marsh. From SR 20 at milepost 42.8, turn north on Rosario Road to find Sharpe County Park on the left in 1.7 miles.

The obvious path leads around a lawn area and reaches the scenic, open water marsh in less than 100 yards, then runs along the shore about 0.2 mile to a junction where a left or right begins a 0.3-

Marsh at Sharpe Park

mile loop. At the far (west) end of the loop, two spurs go to view-points—the right to a small rock bench, the left to a more dramatic place high above the water. After a minor elevation gain, the path emerges into a large rocky meadow with a 180-degree view of paradise (a good place to dive into a long novel). Rosario Head is visible below and to the left, while to the right the San Juan and Gulf Islands are sprawled across the horizon. If you walk toward the water slightly (not too far since there are dangerous cliffs below), you can just see the Deception Pass bridge. Several trail maps with distances noted are posted along the route. The round-trip hike, including the loop and spurs, is just over 1.0 mile.

FIDALGO ISLAND—
18. Rosario Head & Bowman Bay

Distance: 0.5 to 2.3 miles round trip

Time: 1 to 2 hours

Elevation gain: 100 to 200 feet

By itself, the loop around Rosario Head is too short to qualify as much of a hike, but by combining this dramatic coastline with a scoot around Bowman Bay, the trek earns some distinction. For a longer hike, tack on another mile or two while exploring Lottie Bay, Lighthouse Point, and the Canoe Pass overlook nearby (see Hike 19). One can just as well access the latter first and work back to Rosario. The entire area is within Deception Pass State Park. To reach Rosario Beach, follow SR 20 to milepost 42.8 and turn north on Rosario Road, then turn left at the beach sign in 0.8 mile (*see map, p. 92*). The parking area is at the bottom of the hill.

Walk the conspicuous trail through a lawn area to an attractive carving of the Maiden of Deception Pass, guiding spirit of the Samish people. The loop trail splits just ahead with essentially three paths to choose from. The area is too small to get lost in, so just pick one and quickly reach the rocky meadow overlooking Rosario Strait, the

Surge on the rocks below Rosario Head

west entrance to Deception Pass, and West Point, also in the park, but on the other side of the pass (see Hike 59). Deception Island lies to the southwest and Lighthouse Point is to the southeast. There are steep cliffs around much of Rosario Head, but walk to the north side for a picturesque view of jagged rocks and tiny Northwest Island in Rosario Bay. Visit during a gale to watch (carefully) the heavy swell and waves pound against this wild shore.

To reach Bowman Bay, walk back to the lawn area and angle right to a path that gradually rises about 100 feet above the coastline to a point where the trail has been blasted from the cliff. There is a good view of Bowman Bay here. Continue down more steeply to a campground and a short spur to the beach, 0.4 mile from Rosario Bay. One can walk the broad beach 0.5 mile to access a pier or the trails to Lighthouse Point and the Canoe Pass overlook (Hike 19). If walking from Bowman, head up the low bank just before the cliff.

FIDALGO ISLAND—
19. Lighthouse Point & Lottie Bay
Distance: 1.3 to 1.8 miles round trip
Time: 1 to 2 hours
Elevation gain: 100 to 200 feet

It's no secret that some of most dramatic coastline along Washington's inland sea is in the vicinity of Deception Pass, the narrow waterway between Fidalgo and Whidbey Islands, southeast of the San Juans. For most folks it's enough to drive these the islands and experience the rugged beauty of the place through the windshield. Some stop for a photograph, and a few even get out, shake the vertigo, and walk across one or both bridges that span the channel. A few more actually take a hike, and they are the ones who really get to see the place. Several good hikes in the area offer great views of these wild shores, including this little trek to Lighthouse Point and Lottie Bay. The trail is in good shape, but beware of dangerous cliffs (extra caution advised for children and novice hikers).

From I-5, follow SR 20 to MP 47.9 where it turns left. The highway soon skirts Lake Campbell, then Pass Lake. At the end of the latter (milepost 42.8), turn right onto Rosario Road and a quick left to Bowman Bay State Park. Park near the beach, and head for the pier and trail heading left along Bowman Bay. At low tide it's possible to walk the sandy flats around a rock cliff to reach a tombolo beach that connects to what otherwise appears to be an island. If the tide is up, stay on the trail, switchbacking up and over the cliff 0.1 mile to a junction, then head right to the tombolo cross. Lottie Bay is opposite Bowman Bay. As you reenter the forest two paths head up the bank; take the second and angle left. The trail quickly reaches a grassy knoll above the water, where the real beauty begins, 0.5 mile from the start. Both Deception Pass bridges are visible to the left beyond a striking rock fin. A lovely beach awaits on the right.

Continue on the trail past a meadow and follow it through trees to a steep drop-off on the left; Lighthouse Point proper is across the chasm. The Point doesn't offer any particularly striking new views, but for those with the nerve, verve, agility, and ability to go for it, a tall skinny ladder beckons. The less sane among us scramble down

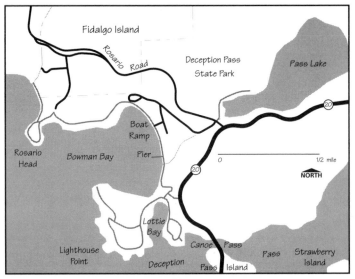

92

Lottie Bay from Canoe Pass overlook

to a tiny beach (unless the tide is very high) and ascend the ladder. Maybe think twice if it's wet, when the metal ladder can be slippery. Wander the trail a bit farther to the next junction where a left turn leads to more great views from a precipitous point. Backtrack to follow the main path to the next junction. Right leads back to the tombolo; left goes to yet another view, from higher cliffs this time. There are a few other unofficial paths in the area, but you will have seen the best of it all by now. So spare the vegetation and stick to the main trail back to the tombolo (connecting) beach.

If you're eager for more, cross the tombolo and ascend a few yards to a junction (left returns to the pier). Turn right to reach the next junction in 0.2 mile and continue straight to ascend switchbacks 0.1 mile to one more viewpoint of Lottie Bay and Deception Pass. Keep walking, then descend on good trail, generally keeping left to complete a short loop back to the tombolo. One spur to the east offers a good view of Canoe Pass, the narrower of the two channels that comprise Deception Pass. More unofficial boot paths can confuse the route, so keep track of your progress and backtrack if necessary. To continue the hike northward around Bowman Bay to Rosario Head, see Hike 18.

Guemes Island
Skagit County

Skagit County's Guemes Island is a placid place. The coastline is not so spectacular as that of some of its neighbors, and there are no super-parks, glistening lakes, or vast stands of old-growth forest to immerse yourself in. But there is a relaxed ambience, and friendly community of islanders on Guemes who seem to enhance the odds of an enjoyable visit. It might not have been so. In the 1960s, a proposed aluminum smelter would have annihilated the island, had it not been for a battle waged and won by a citizens group, Save the San Juans, and their attorney, John Erlichman. Cyclists have since discovered quiet roads and mostly easy grades on Guemes, and footsters have been strolling the beaches for generations. Skip the car entirely and walk or pedal onto the little ferry from Anacortes and enjoy a few happy hours of smelterless islanding. The off season is particularly nice. Note there are both public and private beaches on Guemes, so don't go where you're not wanted.

Guemes Island—
20. Yellow Bluff & Southwest Beach
Distance: 0.5 to 4.0 miles round trip
Time: 1 to 3 hours
Elevation gain: none
Note: Check the tide tables before heading out...

When an easy stroll along an uncrowded beach beckons, try the south shore of Guemes Island, just across the channel from Anacortes. Walk on the ferry then step on the beach and go. If the tide isn't too high, say five feet or less, it may be feasible to walk all the way up the west shore of the Island and beyond. But that is much more beach slogging than most mortals will muster in a day. A creative walk/bike combo can extend the adventure.

Find the Guemes Island Ferry terminal in Anacortes on the northern waterfront, a little west of downtown near Sixth and I

Avenue. The ferry leaves more or less hourly from about six in the morning to around six in the evening Monday through Thursday, then much later in the evening Friday through Sunday. (In early 2001, the fare for a walk-on, with or without a bicycle, was $1.25 round trip.) The cruise is quick—about five minutes. The narrow channel is famous for strong currents that ebb to the west and flood to the east (kayakers beware), which can force the ferry to turn its bow into this veritable river as it scoots across nearly sideways.

From the ferry dock on Guemes, a short walk leads left past homes (or along South Shore Drive) to a bird-rich cattail marsh behind the Southwest Beach, 0.4 mile from the dock. Faint paths approach Demopoulos Marsh, recently acquired by the San Juan Preservation Trust, and a low grassy slope invites a rest in quiet contemplation. Walk the paths if you like, but don't bushwhack. Some of the tidelands on the approach are private, but owners have avoided posting threatening signs. Help maintain the hospitality by not loitering in front of these homes; leaving, taking or disturbing anything; or otherwise making a pest of yourself. Enjoy the beauty, smile neighborly, and move on.

As you round the point, a path leads up a low bank to the west end of South Shore Road, an alternate beach access. Just beyond begins Yellow Bluff, rising abruptly from Southwest Beach. Cypress Island dominates the view to the west across Bellingham Channel.

The shore remains wild for a time, before the bluff recedes and beach homes reappear, about 2 miles from the ferry. Edens Road stops just short of the beach here between houses. A good strategy is to have two or three people walk the beach, while an equal number bicycle from the ferry to this road access. Walkers ride back, and the bikers return to the ferry on foot. Allow at least two hours for the combo, or three hours for the full walk in both directions.

Yellow Bluff up close

James Island

San Juan County

Another of the San Juan's better-known marine recreation getaways is James Island, just off the east shore of Decatur Island. Noted for its "dogbone" shape, the island's two distinct humps rise from a low, narrow middle barely 200 yards across. The middle is where most of the people are since not much else of the island is accessible. Three beaches, campsites, dock, float, mooring buoys, composting toilets and a mile-long loop trail are available to visitors. The island is also known for its pesky racoons, only a bother at night (secure your food well). There are a few deer on the island, one of which we saw being terrorized recently by a careless visitor's unruly dog.

As always, wind and currents are important factors to plan around, especially for the hand- launchers. Nearest put-ins for the latter are at Spencer Spit State Park and the county dock at Hunter Bay, both on Lopez Island. Other boaters reach James from a variety of locations.

James Island by kayak

21. James Island Marine State Park

Distance: 1 mile loop

Time: 1 hour

Elevation gain: 150 feet

A short trail, not quite a mile long, loops around the south lobe of James Island, a marine state park immediately east of Decatur Head in the eastern San Juans. Although some older maps suggest a northern loop, there is little sign of it on the ground. A northerly spur would add considerably to the appeal of James Island, and the state parks agency should seriously consider it, so long as it doesn't compromise the needs of wildlife. People have scrambled up the steep rocky slopes on that end, but the going is rough, potentially dangerous, and only scars the landscape. Instead, walk the south loop, then go find a sunny nook for the eating, reading, and napping part of islanding. There are docks and floats on both the east and west bays, though the floats may be absent in the off-season.

The Southwest Loop Trail is conspicuous and begins above the west bay, climbing through forest to a nice viewpoint at 0.2 mile. A more gradual 0.2-mile descent leads to a little beach and kayakers camp (Cascadia Marine Trail; three sites). A spur continues south a short distance, while the loop heads left past the outhouse, then winds down 0.3 mile to the eastern shore, a 100- yard pea gravel beach between rock ramparts and more campsites. Continue north 0.1 mile to the isthmus, another beach, and more camping. A 50-yard spur leads right to a cliffy overlook with a bench. To extend the day's adventuring, maybe combine the visit to James with a walk on the beach at Decatur Island nearby (see Hike 10).

Jones Island

San Juan County

Just off the west coast of Orcas Island lies 179-acre Jones Island, a popular marine state park with room and reason to linger. About two miles of trails, a couple dozen campsites, a float (seasonal) and dock, beaches, pretty forest, and enchanting rocky shores makes Jones a worthy destination most of the year, with the possible exception of sunny summer weekends when throngs of boaters visit the island. Most visitors, fortunately, zip out not long after zipping in. Those who do linger are well rewarded.

Of course, Jones Island is not served by regular ferry service, but it is easily accessed much of the year by water-taxi from Deer Harbor on Orcas, Friday Harbor on San Juan, and elsewhere. It is also a fairly straightforward paddle for kayakers who often combine Jones with a visit to Yellow Island (Hike 80). The usual hazards of wind and currents occur (currents can get a little tricky for smaller craft). Pleasure boaters can tie up at a float or buoys in North Cove, or buoys at South Cove, while kayakers can land on the gravel beach in a small cove halfway up the west shore. Campsites are at all three locations; summer weekends fill up fast. The west cove camp is part of the Cascadia Marine Trail and is limited to those who arrive by human-powered craft (if landing here, walk the short, signed path to North Cove to find the fee station).

Jones Island—
22. Jones Island Marine State Park

Distance: two 1.0-mile loops
Time: 1 to 2 hours
Elevation gain: 100 to 200 feet

Jones Island offers essentially two loop trails, each about a mile long, one to the northwest and one to the southwest. The west shore is the more scenic part of the island and each loop takes in a portion of it. The Southwest Loop is easy; expect short, steep ups and downs along the Northwest Loop. If beginning at the North Cove dock, walk up through the lawn area to a trail sign where a path on the right leads to the west cove. Or, continue straight ahead on an easy, wide trail, passing windfall from an epic December 1990 storm that blew over many thousands of trees in the islands. Reach South Cove in 0.3 mile (barrier-free to here, though unpaved, and with a gradual hill to climb). A spur to the left leads to another beach and ends. Head right near the shore for the Southwest Loop.

Round a point and begin the lovely west shore, with oak and juniper trees, many rock openings, and good views across the channel to San Juan Island and northwest to Spieden Island's meadowy slopes. Reach a junction near the kayak camp; right leads back to North Cove, or continue straight for the Northwest Loop. Filling the horizon from near the north tip of Jones, lie Spieden, Flattop, Waldron, and Orcas Islands, the Gulf Islands, and part of Sucia Island behind and left of Orcas. The trail climbs moderately to a bench, then descends more steeply to a junction with the North Cove path.

To protect wildlife, including an extraordinarily small variety of deer on Jones Island, Washington State Parks asks that we all stay on designated paths (some older maps show a loop trail on the southeast portion of the island, but it no longer exists). Good well water is usually available at North and South Cove, though it may require boiling and is a source that can run dry by late summer.

Jones Island

Lopez Island

San Juan County

Third largest of the San Juan Islands (29.5 square miles), Lopez Island is also perhaps the most pastoral—the most farmed of all the islands. Lopezians, or Lopezoids if you prefer, are widely regarded as a friendly bunch, exemplified by the Lopez Wave every time one car passes another. If you do not at least lift a finger from the wheel, or one palm from the handlebars, you will be pinpointed instantly as an outsider, which means you're probably just as welcome. Roads are well suited to bicycling, once you've momentarily groaned up the long hill that leaves the ferry dock (avoid Center Road if possible). The urban centroid of Lopez is Lopez Village, a fine place to linger and strategize how to absorb the comfortable pace of island living.

There are no sprawling state or national parks on Lopez, though there are still plenty of wild places to visit, from the famed triangular point at Spencer Spit State Park, to the rugged and storm-battered shores at Shark Reef and Point Colville. Beach walks are a delight on Lopez, and kayakers have been known to spend days exploring the island's intricate coastline. There are good camp-

Upright Channel beach

grounds (and kayak launching) at Spencer Spit and at Odlin County Park, just a mile from the ferry. Lopez is easy to access and normally the first stop on the ferry from Anacortes. The island was named during the first Spanish expedition into the archipelago in 1791 and honors a cohort of explorer Francisco Eliza, Lopez Gonzales de Haro, alleged to have been the first foreigner to set eyes on the islands. Haro Strait immortalizes the same man.

LOPEZ ISLAND—
23. Upright Head to Flat Point
Distance: 1.0 to 3.0 miles round trip

Time: 1 to 2 hours

Elevation gain: none

NOTE: CHECK THE TIDE TABLES BEFORE HEADING OUT...

Odlin County Park, on the northwest shore of Lopez Island, provides the jumping off point for 1.5 miles of beach rambling along Upright Channel, the mile-wide passage between Lopez and Shaw Islands. Although the public shore extends north another mile around Upright Head to the ferry dock, this section is mostly steep rock, much of it impassable even at lower tides. One can also access the beach near Flat Point (described below).

To reach the sandy beach at Odlin Park, walk, bike, or drive 1.2 miles from the ferry dock to the park entrance on the right. Find the beach just ahead and wander left as far as time and tide allow. Fallen trees from the low bluff can block the upper beach in places, so time the walk to avoid the higher tides. The sand is displaced by gravel as you round a point 0.3 mile from the start. Here, Flat Point and its smattering of beachfront homes come into view. The beach returns to sand and remains open and scenic for the duration of the walk. Canoe Island is tucked against Shaw across the channel. Watch for eagles, bay ducks, kingfishers, gulls, and a variety of upland birds, including non-native ring-necked pheasant at Odlin Park. On a May, 2001, kayak outing, we rescued a hypothermic male pheasant in bright, shivering plumage, in the middle of Upright Channel.

About 0.3 mile before Flat Point, a path on the left leads past a sign denoting DNR beach access to Upright Channel. This path emerges from the forest at the north end of a sedge-grass meadow and offers an alternate approach to the beach. To reach this path by road, continue on the Ferry Road 1.5 miles beyond the Odlin Park turnoff, turn right on Military Road, and look for the DNR parking area on the right in 0.3 mile (may be gated in the off-season). There is no camping at this site. A path and service road lead 0.1 mile to restrooms and a picnic area, with a stair-step trail leading 150 yards down to the beach. One can walk past the houses to the end of the public beach, about 0.3 mile south of the point. (Lopez Village is about 1.5 miles farther south, and most of the beach between is public.) The direct ferry between Friday Harbor and Anacortes is something of a spectacle when it passes surprisingly close to Flat Point.

Big Tree/Little Bird

Within Odlin Park, follow the road along the beach into the wooded campground to find the Big Tree Loop and Little Bird Trail just ahead on the left. Big Tree leads across a bridge; stay right for the short loop through an impressive stand of Douglas fir trees four and five feet in diameter. Little Bird bypasses the walk-in campsites, then continues along the bluff to two viewpoints with benches for sitting. Total walking distance for both trails is less than a mile.

LOPEZ ISLAND—

24. Spencer Spit & Lopez Sound

Distance: 0.7 to 5.0 miles round trip

Time: 1 to 3 hours

Elevation gain: minimal

NOTE: CHECK THE TIDE TABLES BEFORE HEADING OUT...

Archaeological studies suggest that the area we know as Spencer Spit on northern Lopez Island was inhabited by Native Americans as long as 3,000 years ago, perhaps as a seasonal or temporary fishing camp. In human terms, three thousand years is a very long time, yet we barely have a clear record of what has transpired in the San Juans over the past 150 years. Since we don't know much about what happened before that, we tend to shrug it off as irrelevant, or not worth bothering with, unless of course you are a Native American—or an archaeologist. While the elders and other experts have pieced together parts of the story of pre-European settlement, there is still no single, assembled history of life in the islands during that era. It won't be an easy task, but hopefully someone will attempt it before long.

For now, we can try to imagine what it was like for the Spencer family to homestead in this area in the 1880s. The land stayed in the family for most of a century, then was acquired by the state for a park in 1967. Interpretive signs and relocated historical cabin on the beach allude to some of that relatively recent history. An upland path through forest explores some of the natural history, but most of the walking is along 3 miles of public beach on either side of the spit and south along Lopez Sound.

To reach Spencer Spit State Park, head south from the ferry dock a mile and turn left on Port Stanley Road. Follow this scenic route about 2.7 miles to Baker View Road; go left again to find the park entrance just ahead. The forest trail crosses the road before reaching the parking area above the spit. Walk left of the restrooms to descend the short distance to the beach. At low tide, one can walk around the entire spit (0.7-mile loop) and the large marsh between the beaches, but stay out of the marsh itself to minimize disturbance to wildlife. On the north side, an entrance channel to the marsh may be bridged with driftwood, though wading is sometimes required to complete the loop. Turn back if necessary.

For a longer trek, continue south along Lopez Sound. The beach transitions to coarse gravel with cobble and boulders much of the way. Uplands are private beyond the park boundary, but the tidelands are public for two miles south of the spit. Across the Sound are Decatur, Trump and Center Islands, left to right. Privately owned Frost Island is just off the end of Spencer Spit, with Blakely Island beyond. To add the forest loop to your journey, walk up the trail leading to the kayakers camp and follow the signs.

Lopez Island—
25. Upright Channel & Fisherman Bay

Distance: 1.4 miles round trip

Time: 1 hour

Elevation gain: none

Note: Check the tide tables before heading out....

At the southwest end of Lopez Island's Fisherman Bay, one can access an excellent sandy beach along the tombolo that separates the bay from San Juan Channel. Only a small parking area is provided, two skips from the beach. To find it, follow Ferry Road and Fisherman Bay Road south from the ferry dock, past Lopez Village and around the bay. At six miles from the dock, turn right on Bayshore Road and find the parking area on the left in 0.6 mile.

The beach to the south is private, though locals have enjoyed the stroll to the big boulder and beyond for generations. The tombolo beach to the north is public. One can walk the beach facing San Juan Channel for about 0.7 mile to a parking area at the north end. The upper beach is mostly sand, but lower areas are coarse round gravel. The low green meadow across the channel is part of San Juan Island's American Camp. The Olympic Mountains trace the skyline beyond, and Shaw Island lies to the north. The inside shore along Fisherman Bay is private, with marsh and mudflats at lower tides that make it more attractive to great blue herons than people.

Lopez Island—
26. Shark Reef Sanctuary

Distance: 0.6 mile round trip

Time: 1 to 2 hours

Elevation gain: minimal

Short hike. Big views. If an easy hike to a scenic rocky shore is on the agenda, the former military reserve at Shark Reef is an excellent choice. But don't expect to see any sharks, or even Shark Reef, a shoal that is just offshore but too far north to be seen from the path.

Instead, enjoy the walk in forest to a picturesque coastline near the turbulent south entrance to San Juan Channel. The Cattle Point Lighthouse and American Camp are barely a mile away, with the vast Strait of Juan de Fuca beyond. Strong currents can develop with a big tide exchange, a veritable river in the sea.

Parking is extremely limited, so maybe plan on cycling there if your visit happens on a fair weather weekend. From Lopez Village, head south on Fisherman Bay Road about 3 miles to Airport Road; turn right, then left on Shark Reef Road to find the trailhead 1.8 miles ahead on the right. (No camping; pets on a leash; trail closed to bikes.) Two paths merge in 100 yards (the left is easier). Continue 0.2 mile to the rocky bluff whre a path weaves southward along the shore past good sitting rocks, ending at a private fence line in 200 yards. Seals and sea lions often bask offshore at Deadman Island and on surrounding rocks, and orcas occasionally slip by close to shore. Deep water and upwelling currents make this a rich feeding area for a marine life. Eagles are a common sight as well.

Rock scramblers can work north along the shore at lower tides to reach a pocket beach in 200 yards (with homes above). Note that the uplands here are private. Although public tidelands extend another 1.5 miles northward, the next section is steep and impassable. Do not trespass. During fall and winter storms, the coast here offers a lively scene of crashing surf (bundle up and hang on!).

Shark Reef

LOPEZ ISLAND—
27. Watmough Bay & Point Colville
Distance: 0.5 to 1.5 miles

Time: 1 to 2 hours

Elevation gain: minimal

The exposed southern coast of Lopez Island is remarkably different from the more placid shores of the northern portion. Reefs, rocks and small islands are strewn along the ragged shore from Shark Reef eastward to Watmough Head and beyond. Most of the coast is privately owned, however, and hiking opportunities are fairly limited. Point Colville and Watmough Bay offer small windows into this little paradise and are worth a visit almost anytime. (Some maps show, correctly, a large block of public land at Iceberg Point as well, but there is no overland access easement to that area for the general

public.) At Watmough Head, the U.S. Bureau of Land Management (BLM) and the San Juan County Land Bank co-manage substantial acreage that does provide for public access. Other than an outhouse, there are no facilities, so pack out whatever you pack in and treat this place as the fragile ecological reserve that it is.

From Center Road or Fisherman Bay Road, head south to Mud Bay Road, then follow this 4 miles and

Watmough Beach

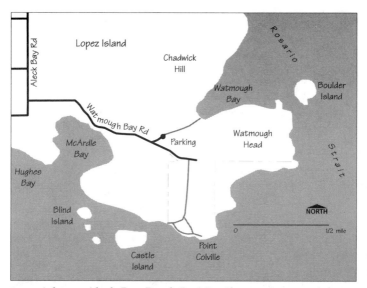

turn right on Aleck Bay Road. In 0.5 mile, continue straight on Watmough Bay Road which bends to the east; less than a mile farther angle left to the parking area. The obvious path leads past an outhouse about 0.2 mile to the beach. The scenic pea-gravel beach is only 150 yards long and abuts rock walls and boulders at each end. Chadwick Hill (mostly DNR land) rises to the north (left) and the small bay rounds Watmough Head to the right. Boulder Island just offshore is part of the National Wildlife Refuge and is off-limits. Mount Baker looms in the distance.

To enjoy the view at Point Colville, return to the parking area and walk out to the road junction to go left. Follow the road up a rising curve to enter BLM land and find the trail on the right 50 yards before a private road signed "no trespassing" (parking is discouraged here). Walk the easy path through open forest and go left or right at a fork to complete a short loop. A large, open rocky meadow overlooks the Strait of Juan de Fuca. Castle Island is to the right: a steep, protected island of the National Wildlife Refuge. A wood fence across from the island marks the end of public land.

Matia Island

San Juan County

The northernmost islands in the San Juan archipelago lie due north of Orcas Island: Matia, Sucia, Patos and many more rocks and islets. Each is heavily forested and made of 40 to 80-million-year-old sandstone sculpted by wind, waves, and sea salt. All three were named during the Eliza expedition in the 1790s, and except for the caretaker's quarters on Sucia, all three remain uninhabited, despite a sizeable summer boating population. All three are marine state parks. Sucia is the largest, and by far, the most popular of the three; Matia is the smallest, and Patos the least visited (it lacks a dock). Each is plenty scenic, hiker friendly, and well worth a visit.

Matia, the easterly of the three, is a slender mile long and only 145 acres. Still, it is one of the larger islands of the San Juan Islands National Wildlife Refuge, and one of only two in the refuge that are accessible to the public (Turn Island is the other; see Hike 58). However, only a five-acre portion, including the campground and beach area, are within the state park. The rest is both refuge and designated wilderness. Except for the trails, these protected areas are off limits to humans in order to protect sensitive birds and marine mammals. Several small coves on the south shore and at the east end are attractive to kayakers, but keep in mind that the northern and eastern portions should not be approached any closer than 200 yards.

Matia Island—
28. Matia Island Loop

Distance: 1.0 to 1.5 miles round trip

Time: 1 hour

Elevation gain: 200 feet

From a distance, Matia Island appears like any other: a rounded tree-covered knob, aloof on the watery horizon. But up close, Matia is a little dreamland with rugged sandstone shores and an interior of mostly old-growth forest. The entire island is within the

San Juan Islands National Wildlife Refuge (NWR). At Rolfe Cove on the north side, Washington State Parks maintains a boat dock and float, a few mooring buoys, campsites, odor-free composting toilets, and a scenic 1.0-mile loop trail among big trees.

Boaters should be alert to odd currents that flow through the cove. Also, the float is absent during the winter months due to rough conditions. While visiting the island once in late winter, we tied up to a buoy and rowed to shore in a tiny dinghy. On the way back, a surprisingly strong current almost swept us past the boat and into Georgia Strait—beware! Of historical interest, in the winter of 1921, Elvin Smith, the island hermit, disappeared with his rowboat somewhere between Matia and Orcas Islands, at the youthful age of 86. Evidence of the old man's homestead has nearly vanished.

A kiosk above the pebbly beach explains the rules: stay on the trail and leave the place better than you found it. Matia is very much a wildlife-sensitive place. The loop begins just behind the sign near a big rock wall. The path climbs gently among giant firs, cedars, and car-sized boulders in a setting similar to the Chuckanut Mountains south of Bellingham. Soon enough the trail slopes down to a narrow bay at the southeast end of the island and a beach trail junction, 0.4 mile from the start. Just beyond, a spur heads 0.25 mile left along the outer shore of the small penisula that encloses the bay. A few drop-offs and slick spots warrant extra caution. Back at the junction, continue through smaller trees that hint of Elvin's small-time agrarian use of the area many years ago. Sharp eyes may notice leaning fenceposts, barbed wire, and decaying boards of a small, collapsed building. Pass another scenic cove and little cattail marsh on the return to Rolfe Cove. Allow plenty of time to linger.

Matia Island cove

Orcas Island

San Juan County

Vancouver's sister ship, the H.M.S. Chatham, made a brush with the rocks on the southeast shore of Orcas Island in 1792. A century later, more than a hundred settlers were carving a livelihood into the island's forested shores and valleys. Today, Orcas accounts for about one-third of the population of San Juan County, with about 4,500 year-round residents. At 58 square miles, Orcas Island is barely the largest of the San Juans (San Juan is 57). Its shape is as distinct as any other, with two broad arms wrapped around the six-mile-long inlet of East Sound. At the head of the inlet is the town of Eastsound, the second-largest community in San Juan County. A second large bay, West Sound, extends three miles into the westerly arm, and yet another, Deer Harbor, immediately to the west, incises this smaller peninsula. As a result, the island boasts more than 50 miles of the county's 375 miles of saltwater shoreline.

Washington's fourth largest state park, Moran State Park, is found on the eastern arm. The park's 5,000 acres of forest and lakes offer more miles of trails, by far, than any other island in the county. On the downside, there are almost no public trails on Orcas outside the park, and very little public access to the extensive shoreline surrounding the island. In terms of parks and water access, Orcas Island comes in a distant second to the diversity of sites and environments available to the public on San Juan Island. Nevertheless, Moran is a superb place to hit the trail. What it lacks in marine waterfront, it makes up in loop trails around two large lakes—Cascade and Mountain. Waterfalls and old-growth forest add interest to the hike between the two lakes. And the complete ascent to the summit of Mount Constitution—highest point in the islands—is comparable to a modest hike in the Olympics or North Cascades. Despite the popular paved road that climbs to within a few yards of the summit, a brisk hike up the mountain is a must for any serious footster. Eight hikes in the park are listed below.

Orcas Island is easily reached by ferry, although the ferry dock at the entrance to West Sound is a long way from any park or public beach access. Cyclists will find hilly, winding roads over much of the island, making day trips to Moran State Park more of challenge than most other islands. Boaters, on the other hand, will find much to explore and plenty of reasons to return.

<small>ORCAS ISLAND—</small>
29. Eastsound & Madrona Point
Distance: 1 to 4.5 miles round trip

Time: 1 to 3 hours

Elevation gain: minimal

At the head of Orcas Island's East Sound, a small peninsula, Madrona Point, divides Ship Bay from Fishing Bay, with the historic Eastsound community gathered around the latter. The community is small and quaint, a popular tourist stop, and easily explored on foot. One could park anywhere and perhaps head for the excellent historical museum highlighting both native and nonnative culture. If some extra walking is on the agenda, find a new path heading north to the airport and North Beach. Begin near the post office, a couple of blocks north and west of the museum (turn right at the airport, and left on North Beach Road). Otherwise, amble your way through town, then head for the Point.

Known as "Tsel Whi'sen" by Native Americans, Madrona Point was nearly lost to developers in the late 1980s. The point was ultimately spared and acquired for conservation through the efforts of the Lummi Tribe and others. The Lummi's have been generous enough to allow access to the public (day-use only). It is a spiritually significant place to them, so leave no trace when you visit. No bikes, no pets, no fires, no digging.

If coming from the ferry landing, follow the signs into Eastsound and turn right on Haven Road as you reach the end of the main business district. The parking area is just ahead. The trail is obvious and generally easy to follow, though several forks can be a bit brushy. Ample madrona trees explain the place name, joined by Douglas fir and juniper trees as well. A small open meadow above the shore affords a nice view of Ship Bay and Mount Constitution.

Orcas Island—
30. Cascade Lake & Rosario Lagoon

Distance: 2.7 to 5.6 mile loop
Time: 2 to 5 hours
Elevation gain: 100 to 800 feet

When the weather is good, Orcas Island's second largest lake can be a very popular place. A scenic shoreline and easy access next to the Horseshoe Highway in Moran State Park can't help but attract picnickers, campers, swimmers, pedal-boaters, paddlers, birdwatchers, loungers, restroom seekers, and hikers in fair numbers from late spring to early fall. If the crowds don't bug you, have at it anytime. Or, if you would rather enjoy a little more of the lake to yourself, go in the off-season, pick a less than perfect summer day, or lace up the boots after an early breakfast. This lake is worth the walk—and maybe a swim from one of many rocky perches around the lake. The basic loop is 2.7 miles long, but several good side-trips can more than double the distance. Note there are some cliffy areas that may require extra attention with younger kids.

From the ferry dock, it's 13 miles to the parking area adjacent to

Cascade Lake

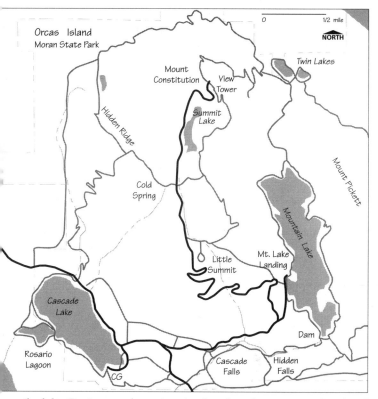

the lake. Begin near the swimming beach and restrooms, then head right for a counterclockwise circuit. Pass a few well designed interpretive signs and look for the path close to shore. Most of the way wends through trees close to water, with good views almost from start to finish. The northern and western shores are also pretty and interesting to walk. At various junctions with other paths and roads, it's fairly obvious where to go to continue around the lake.

About midway along the loop the trail splits at Rosario Lagoon (quite visible through trees). The main lake loop heads up and left, or take the right fork for a 0.7 mile (one-way) walk along the north side of the lagoon—a skinny arm of the lake that was created when a small dam was built to supply power to what is now the Rosario Resort. The dam also expanded Cascade Lake considerably. If taking the Rosario trail, turn left when you meet a road, then left again on a path next to a tennis court. At the dam you can either retrace your steps or continue on a steep route down to the resort (adding another 1.4 miles and 350-foot elevation loss and gain).

If the resort beckons, walk the road left a few paces to a precipitous path down a ravine; go left on pavement then right on a gravel drive through a maintenance area, then left on a paved road around the bend (right) to another wide path leading down the bluff to the resort and marina. Walk around a pond and the marina and stay close to the water to pick up a sidewalk that leads directly to the impressive Rosario mansion. The route is partly signed for resort guests who wish to make the ascent to Cascade Lake (for the return, aim for the three-story building with all the skinny windows). At the lagoon, it's possible to wander the south shore back to Cascade Lake, but the going is rough and potentially brushy.

Back at the Cascade Lake-Rosario Lagoon junction mentioned earlier, a left leads 150 yards along a rocky rib to an attractive log bridge and some fine rock to lounge away the day. Pass the south side lagoon trail and walk the next 0.6 mile mostly in trees with limited views. Where the trail meets a campground, another good side trip goes to Sunrise Rock, 0.4 mile and 350 feet above the lake (well signed). For this one, climb 0.1 mile to a junction, head right, then soon begin the short steep switchbacks taking you to a slabby rock outcrop with a decent view of the lake below (dangerous cliffs close by). On a clear day, Three Fingers Mountain in the North Cascades is visible to the southeast.

To finish the loop, walk east through the campground to pick up the trail again near its entrance. Follow the lakeshore, then turn right at a paved path, left on a road, then right to find the signed path again across the main highway (watch for traffic). Climb a bit, go left at a junction, jog right on a road, then left again (more signs) to complete the loop near the swimming beach. The lake and lagoon are good for birding early in the year. Watch for ring-necked ducks, hooded mergansers, bald eagles, and osprey, among others.

ORCAS ISLAND—
31. Cascade Creek & Falls

Distance: 0.4 to 7.0 miles round trip

Time: 1 to 3 hours

Elevation gain: minimal to 700 feet

This 3.0-mile hike along Cascade Creek between Cascade and Mountain Lakes is appealing for both a series of waterfalls (best viewed fall through spring) and some of the largest trees anywhere in the islands—Douglas firs up to six feet in diameter. The hike can be done one-way, uphill or downhill, with a lift back to the other end, or round trip as one or two meandering loops that meet in the middle as described below. The trail also serves as a link in a more ambitious around-the-mountain tour (see Hike 36). Or, one can simply walk 0.4 mile to Cascade and Rustic Falls and return from the intermediate trailhead. The option described here begins at this trailhead, though the route can easily be adapted to begin at Mountain Lake Landing or the South End Campground at Cascade Lake.

From Cascade Lake at milepost 13 on the Horseshoe Highway, continue east and angle left on the road leading up Mount Constitution. Park at the well-signed trailhead on the right (*map, p. 113*). Follow the right-hand path down to the falls, then aim for the lower viewpoint and the bridge across the creek. Having enjoyed the view, cross the bridge and take a left at the next junction. In about 0.5 mile go left on the old road leading up Mount Pickett (see Hike 37). Descend on this briefly to the Mountain Lake junction near Hidden Falls. It's about 0.9 mile from here to the lake and 0.6 mile farther to Mountain Lake Landing. Either cross the footbridge and ascend to the lake and return, or continue down the old road to a fork on the left leading past Cavern Falls and Rustic Falls before arriving back at Cascade Falls 0.7 mile from the Mountain Lake junction. Use caution at the top of Cascade Falls where the trail passes very close to the brink. This upper loop is about 1.8 miles long.

For the lower loop, return to the parking area, cross the road and follow the obvious path about 0.7 mile to a junction. Turn left on a narrow path, ambling back down to the Horseshoe Highway at its intersection with the road leading to the South End Campground on Cascade Lake. Follow this road to a paved path on the right which leads to an unpaved path that parallels the lake shore briefly before reaching the campground. Turn right and walk to the gate at the end of the camp area, about 1.2 miles from the intermediate trailhead (see Hike 30 for a loop around Cascade Lake). At the gate, head left up the hill 0.1 mile to the next junction; turn left again and follow this through attractive forest and a stand of very large Douglas firs. Watch for an unusually large Sitka spruce on the right. Stay right and drop slightly at the next fork, reaching a paved road about 0.7 mile from the campground. Cross to a good trail through more old growth reaching Cascade Falls once again in 0.2 mile. A left leads back to the trailhead to complete the 2.1 mile lower loop.

ORCAS ISLAND—
32. Mountain Lake & Twin Lakes

Distance: 3.6 to 6.2 miles round trip

Time: 2 to 4 hours

Elevation gain: 300 feet

Mountain Lake and Cascade Lake at Moran State Park are the largest lakes in the San Juan Islands, and both offer scenic loop trails around their shores (see Hike 30 for the Cascade Lake loop). Mountain Lake is the longer trek, and an attractive side-trip leads to Big and Little Twin Lakes nearby. Many prefer to walk the loop counterclockwise for better views of Mount Constitution. The wide path along the west shore makes an easy stroll.

For directions to the lake, see Hike 33 (*map, p. 113*). From Mountain Lake Landing, head right from the parking area to pick up the trail and stay left at a junction (right leads back to the road). At 0.6 mile, the trail reaches the small earthen dam at the lake's outlet and a junction with the Cascade Creek Trail on the right and the Mount Pickett Trail just beyond (see Hikes 31 and 37). The next section passes through impressive forest with a number of Douglas fir trees exceeding five feet in diameter. The steep east face of Mount Con-

Mountain Lake

stitution dominates the view at several openings in the trees. This is the best part of the walk so a little foot-dragging may be in order.

At about 2.3 miles, the trail reaches the head of Mountain Lake and the junction to Twin Lakes. It's another 0.8 mile to a spur on the right leading to the loop trails around Big and Little Twin Lakes (0.6 and 0.4 mile respectively). The north end of the Mount Pickett Trail intersects the Little Twin loop. Both loops are easy, though the paths are not as well maintained. From the head of Mountain Lake, the main trail leads back to the Landing in 1.3 miles.

ORCAS ISLAND—
33. Mt. Constitution from Mountain Lake

Distance: 3.5 to 5.5 miles one way

Time: 2 to 4 hours

Elevation gain: 1,500 feet

Driving to the summit of Mount Constitution in Moran State Park is, for some, like eating the frosting without enjoying the cake. The hike up the east side of the mountain is definitely one for the cake eaters. There a several good routes up the mountain, though the approach from Mountain Lake is appealing because you can actually see what you're climbing—and it's an impressive sight. As you head up the trail, there's a distinct feeling of being somewhere in the Cascades or Olympics, en route to a lonely summit. Unfortunately, if the weather is fair, the summit will most likely be anything but lonely. Still, the trek does provide a fine winter or spring substitute when the aforementioned ranges are buried in winter snowpack. The 2.8-mile descent via Little Summit makes an excellent circuit (see Hike 34 for details).

From the Orcas Island ferry landing, follow the signs to Eastsound and on to the Moran State Park entrance, 13 miles from the dock. Continue past Cascade Lake, ignore the turn for Olga, and take the next right to Mountain Lake Landing (map, p. 113). Park near the lakeshore (well signed). The shortest approach to the summit heads left past a campground, but the more scenic hike around the east side of Mountain Lake heads right and adds about 1.0 mile. Either way, the walk to the lake's north end is easy and generally close to water. If doing the shorter route, reach the junction to Twin Lakes at 1.3 miles, or 2.3 miles the long way. The latter passes a small dam at 0.6 mile where a trail leads down Cascade Creek (see Hike 31); a second trail just beyond heads up Mount Pickett (Hike 37).

From the junction at the north end of Mountain Lake, it is 0.8 mile to the next junction at Twin Lakes (see Hike 32). Head right to explore these two gems (the two short loops would add almost 1.0 mile of walking), or continue on the main trail for the summit, pass-

Twin Lakes and Rosario Strait from Mt. Constitution

ing the other end of the Big Twin Loop nearby. Stay left at this junction and left again in 0.3 mile (the other trail makes a long loop around the north side of the mountain to Hidden Ridge and Cold Spring; see Hike 36). At this point the path immediately begins a series of moderately steep switchbacks on the final mile to the top. Look for a spur trail on the left at a signed switchback and follow this down slightly 150 yards to a good view of the precipitous east face of Mount Constitution. Back on the summit trail, it's another 0.7 mile to the trail's end at the summit road. Head left up the road and aim for the obvious view tower. Now, enjoy the frosting: Sucia and Matia Islands to the north, Barnes, Clark, and Lummi Islands to the northeast, Bellingham and Mount Baker to the east, and Cypress and Guemes Islands to the southeast. Twin Lakes and Mountain Lake are nestled in the plush green carpet below.

ORCAS ISLAND—
34. Mt. Constitution from Little Summit
Distance: 2.3 miles one way

Time: 1 to 2 hours

Elevation gain: 500 feet

Little Summit offers an easy route to the true summit of Mount Constitution, and it makes a good descent route for a climb up from Cascade or Mountain Lakes. Either way, the trail takes in some of the best the mountain has to offer. If using this as a descent route after going up a different way, see the note at the end of this listing. The description below is from Little Summit up to the view tower at the true summit. Salal and manzanita crowd the trail high on the ridge, while more densely forested ground is found near Summit Lake. Find the Little Summit Trailhead at a small turn-out on the right along the Mount Constitution Road, about 3.0 miles above its intersection with the road to Olga (*map, p. 113*).

From the parking area, walk 50 yards to a junction and head

Mt. Constitution's summit ridge

right and up 100 yards to the site of the former fire lookout. Here, you can enjoy a view of Lopez Island and the Olympics that you won't see from the summit tower. Return to the junction and turn right, cross a small creek, and descend slightly to reach the next junction in 0.2 mile (a right here descends 0.8 mile to Mountain Lake Landing). Head left to another junction in a short mile, as the route begins to climb. Left here leads to Cold Spring, but stay right for 0.2 mile and watch for a short spur on the left going to the edge of placid Summit Lake. The main trail soon breaks into the open for increasingly wider views over the last 0.8 mile to the true summit and unique stone tower built in the 1930s by the Civilian Conservation Corps.

On the descent, find the trail heading south from the tower. Stay left in 1.0 mile at the Cold Spring junction beyond Summit Lake. If completing a loop from Mountain and Twin Lakes, hike another mile and go left again at the 0.8-mile spur to Mountain Lake Landing, reaching the latter 2.8 miles from the summit. The spur is moderately steep; stay on the path where it touches a bend in the road to find the Landing just ahead. (A right at the Cold Spring junction and a left 0.3 mile beyond will take you to Cascade Lake.)

ORCAS ISLAND—
35. Mt. Constitution from Cascade Lake
Distance: 4.2 miles one way

Time: 2 to 3 hours

Elevation gain: 2,100 feet

The trek with the most elevation gain up Mount Constitution begins at Cascade Lake. The route ascends Cold Creek and finishes via the Little Summit Trail. Or, for those fellow trail gluttons who prefer harder routes over easy, the ascent can be directed around the north side of the mountain to link with the route going up from Twin Lakes (for that, see Hikes 33 and 36). Begin the Cold Creek hike at the information kiosk and trailhead opposite Cascade Lake, just before the milepost 13 marker. One can also include this route in a loop to Little Summit, Mountain Lake, and Cascade Creek (see

Mount Baker from Mount Constitution

Hikes 31 and 34; *map, p. 113*).

The trail passes a giant cedar tree next to the creek and begins to climb, crossing Cold Creek several times, and passing large firs while ascending a long series of switchbacks. Rocky openings and an old mineshaft near the 2.0-mile point offer brief diversions from the long, upward trudge. The mineshaft is just above the trail and below a rock wall, and is just long enough to require a light; beware of loose and falling rock if you decide to venture inside—part of the mine has caved in; if you skip it, you haven't missed much.

Continue up 0.4 mile to a junction, having gained about 1,700 feet from Cascade Lake. Hidden Ridge is to the left. Turn right to reach Cold Spring in 0.5 mile and easier going beyond. The spring once provided water to a campground nearby that has since been converted to a picnic area. Walk by it just before you cross the Mount Constitution Road. Reach the Little Summit Trail 0.3 mile from Cold Spring (3.2 miles from Cascade Lake). Head left here for the last leisurely mile, mostly along an open ridge, to the summit tower.

ORCAS ISLAND—
36. Hidden Ridge & North Side Trail

Distance: 3.9 miles one way (or more)

Time: 2 hours (or more)

Elevation gain: 700-foot descent

Hidden Ridge is appropriately named; it lies somewhat off the beaten track, which makes it a good place to head for a less-peopled summer hike in Moran State Park. The rounded ridge crest is only a few hundred feet below the summit of Mount Constitution, but unfortunately, lacks the amazing views found along the true summit ridge. If a more remote trek in the park beckons, consider hiking Hidden Ridge and a long trail around the north side of the mountain that eventually connects with the trail heading up from Twin Lakes. Parts of the trail can be a little brushy at times, depending on how recently things were trimmed back. A pleasant, over-the-top, 6.2-mile loop involves continuing up to the summit from the Twin Lakes area, and descending via the Little Summit Trail to the Cold Spring Trail. The loop entails a 700-foot descent, followed by a 1,000-foot climb, and another descent of 300 feet—1,000 feet up and 1,000 down (one would think the up and the down would cancel each other out, but somehow, for the legs involved, they don't).

From the Horseshoe Highway, head up the Mount Constitution Road 3.7 miles to the Cold Spring Picnic Area on the left. Hike the trail about 0.2 mile to Cold Spring and another 0.5 mile to the junction with the Hidden Ridge Trail (left descends steeply to Cascade Lake; see Hike 35). Continue along the gentle ridge past a marsh and several small ponds, then descend slightly to pass a small lake surrounded by private property. The route soon bends to the east, crosses an old road (also private), then descends more across the steep mountainside, eventually meeting the trail near Twin Lakes, 3.4 miles from the Cold Creek–Hidden Ridge junction. Unless you're headed for Twin Lakes or Mountain Lake Landing, head right for the final steep mile to the summit. From the top, follow the Little Summit Trail 1.0 mile down to the Cold Spring Trail junction; the parking area is about 0.25 mile to the right (*map, p. 113*).

ORCAS ISLAND—
37. Mount Pickett
Distance: 6.4-mile loop

Time: 3 to 4 hours

Elevation gain: 900 feet

For those who have hiked everything else at Moran State Park but still need to break in their boots, the long trek over Mount Pickett may be just the thing. There are only limited views and no particular destination to drool over, but the woods are nice enough. It makes sense to do the hike as a loop, using the Mountain Lake Trail for one leg, either coming or going. Theoretically, the Mount Pickett Trail begins at Cascade Creek near Hidden Falls and ends at Little Twin Lake, but it might make more sense to begin and end the loop at Mountain Lake Landing. Either direction works fine.

From Mountain Lake Landing (see Hike 33 for directions), head left along the shore 1.3 miles to the lake's north end and the Twin Lakes Trail junction; turn left. In 0.8 mile more, go right and right again around Little Twin Lake to the signed Mount Pickett Trail on the right. This trail widens to an old road as it climbs steadily for about 1.6 miles to the summit, a 500-foot elevation gain from Twin Lakes. Skip the path on the left and follow the old road down the south slope, staying right at the next three junctions. The third right leads to the south end of Mountain Lake a short distance from the dam—about 2.0 miles from the summit. Head left across Cascade Creek, and walk the last easy 0.6 mile back to the Landing.

Orcas Island—
38. Obstruction Pass

Distance: 1.4 miles round trip
Time: 1 to 2 hours
Elevation gain: minimal

A bit off the beaten path, DNR's Obstruction Pass recreation site is better known as a walk-in or kayakers campground (part of the Cascadia Marine Trail), but it makes an easy dayhike as well. Two beaches, south- and west-facing, demand some lingering, and the mature forest makes a pleasant camp. If spending the night, try to arrive by early afternoon, or time your visit mid- week or off-season to improve the odds of finding a good site. My own brief visits to Obstruction Pass in early spring have been rewarded with copious bird life and few boaters.

From the Orcas ferry landing, head for Moran State Park and keep going, following the signs to Olga. Turn left on Point Lawrence Road, about 17 miles from the ferry dock. Turn right just ahead on Obstruction Pass Road, then stay right on the signed gravel road that leads to the parking area and trailhead at its end. The hike is straightforward for 0.5 mile to a fork; continue straight to pass out-houses and several campsites close to the south beach. Wander right here (or at the fork) through open forest to a small headland with cozy beaches on either side. Note that the south tip of the peninsula is signed private. Obstruction Pass is hidden to the east where boats seem to emerge from nowhere, while at night the ferries' floating masses of lights drift in and out of the Lopez Island dock three miles to the southwest.

West cove, near Obstruction Pass Campground

Patos Island

San Juan County

Ine of the most remote islands of the San Juans, Patos is the westerly island of a group of three outliers north of Orcas and within full view of Canada. Like its more immediate neighbors, Sucia and Matia, Patos' shores are predominantly rugged sandstone sculpted by wind, waves, salt, and time. The smallish island is heavily forested except at the northwest end where an historic lighthouse stands above barren rock and a wildflower meadow. The lighthouse is now automated and Patos has been converted to a marine state park with a handful of campsites, an outhouse, a couple of mooring buoys, and a mile-long loop trail. An islet helps contain the harbor and adds to the beauty. Its remoteness generally means fewer visitors, though sunny summer weekends can get a little crazy almost anywhere in the islands

Patos Island—
39. Patos Island Marine State Park

Distance: 1.5-mile loop (plus walkable beaches)

Time: 1 to 3 hours

Elevation gain: 100 feet

Far less visited than neighboring Sucia, Patos Island offers much of the same beauteous coastline, with several miles of walkable bedrock and gravel shore (except at higher tides). A 1.5-mile loop circles half the island and a 0.2-mile spur leads to the lighthouse. Getting to Patos, like the other more remote islands, can be challenging to small boaters, with potentially dangerous currents, tide rips, and open exposure to Georgia Strait and Boundary Pass. There are good campsites on the island and a fairly well protected harbor—Active Cove—on the west end, but no dock.

From the obvious beach at the head of Active Cove, pick up the signed loop trail near the information kiosk (with picnic tables, outhouses, and campsites nearby). A clockwise hike is described here,

Patos Island

though if walking in the morning light, reversing the route may be more scenic. Head left on a good trail to a junction, passing several camping and picnic sites with views of the cove; the loop turns right but continue toward the left to a concrete sidewalk (of all things). Left again goes to an old dock gradually being reclaimed by sea; right leads a hundred yards to the former lighthouse compound and two large buildings about to disappear in brush. The photogenic, boarded-up lighthouse is just ahead near the tip of Alden Point.

From Alden Point, one can begin a wild walk and scramble eastward along Patos' northern bedrock shore. Unless the tide is very high, essentially the entire length of the island (1.5 miles) can be negotiated by most hikers. But some backtracking will be necessary to regain the loop trail which does not run the length of the island. If walking the trail, return to the junction just before the sidewalk and turn left to make the short crossing to the north shore. The path parallels the shore for about 0.5 mile before turning inland again at a long gravel beach. If taking the bedrock beach route from the lighthouse, watch for the trail just above the rocks after a half-mile or so. The path winds through a lovely forest to the south shore not far from the start.

San Juan Island

San Juan County

A gaggle of good hiking is found on the archipelago's namesake land mass, San Juan Island. Well known for many things—for its historical importance in the settlement of the international boundary with Canada; for its scenic urban center and county seat, Friday Harbor; for its pastoral uplands and dramatic coastline; for its biking, hiking and whale-watching opportunities; for its museums, resorts, parks, and natural areas; for its slow-lane lifestyle and friendly residents. One can wonder why we all don't live there (it's a good thing we don't). Development pressures are ever-rising in the islands. Yet San Juan has managed to sustain its endemic charm and visitor appeal despite occasional losses to the land speculators.

In summer, San Juan Island is a heavy favorite for ferry travelers, for all the reasons noted above. Fortunately, the island is large and people can spread out, though expect the best places to get crowded, especially on the weekends. Like anywhere else, however, most folks tend to hang close to the cars and nearer to visitor comforts; so to break loose from the droves, simply wander up a trail or beach for a half-mile, or farther for a chance at solitude. Or, travel in less than perfect weather, go midweek, or save your rambling for the off-season, typically mid-September to mid- May. Do the same to avoid the long ferry lines, or leave the car in Anacortes and bike from there. Most of San Juan is reasonably bike friendly, and though shoulders are lacking on many routes, drivers are generally courteous. Bikes, mopeds, and the like can be rented in Friday Harbor, and water taxis will take you just about anywhere for a fee. Sorry to say, boaters will find crowded harbors and moorages in summer as well. This is less of a problem for kayakers who can sneak into places that no one else can. Refer to the usual boating guides for more information.

San Juan Island—
40. English Camp & Bell Point

Distance: 1 to 2 miles round trip

Time: 1 hour (or more)

Elevation gain: minimal (some steep short hills)

Historic English Camp on the north end of San Juan Island is a popular stop for island visitors, and offers a pleasant self-guided interpretive walk just under a mile in length, with an optional loop around Bell Point for an added mile of coastal exploring. Garrison Bay's protected waters and strategic location made this not only a good place from which to defend the British Crown's claim to the islands in the mid-1800s, but an ideal wintering camp for the Native Americans that preceded the British. An enormous mound of discarded shells (or midden) observed by the newcomers offered evidence of the natives' ongoing subsistence on shellfish at the site over countless generations. Perhaps someday the park brochure will illuminate some of that history, but for now, the emphasis is on the unusual story of the famed "pig incident" of the 1860s which help settle a long-standing boundary dispute between Canada and the U.S. (see the introductory section, About the Islands).

From Friday Harbor, reach this northerly unit of San Juan Island National Historical Park via Roche Harbor Road (watch for signs after departing the ferry). About nine miles from the ferry dock, turn left on West Valley Road. The park is 1.5 miles ahead on the right. Begin the walk at the lower corner of the parking lot and grab a pamphlet for the guided tour. Head right at the first junction,

Canadian honkers at English Camp

descend and pass the old barracks and two giant big leaf maple trees, then the blockhouse next to the beach. Find the Bell Point Loop beginning and ending near the pear trees.

For the latter, one can walk 0.5 mile on a good trail to the Point through madrona, fir, and juniper forest, or wander along the beach if the tide's not too high, although the tideflats can be mucky in places. Near Bell Point, a spur leads left to the low rock shelf overlooking Westcott Bay which shares its narrow entrance channel with Garrison Bay. Watch for Indian paintbrush and other wildflowers blooming in the spring. Retrace the spur trail, head left, then right at the next two junctions to return to the camp. From the blockhouse, the interpretive walk passes through an impressive privet-hedge garden, then steeply up steps to the site of the commanding officers' quarters. A monument to the boundary settlement stands nearby. The loop ends just ahead near the parking lot.

San Juan Island—
41. Mount Young
Distance: 1.5 miles round trip

Time: 1 hour

Elevation gain: 700 feet

One of San Juan Island's better known and often trekked trails is Mount Young from English Camp. Open, rocky meadows at the summit offer sweeping views of San Juan Island and its neighbors to the west and north, including B.C.'s Vancouver and Gulf Islands. Spring wildflowers add a noteworthy charm, including chocolate and white fawn lilies, camas, shooting stars, and more. Spring and summer are also good for viewing turkey vultures, chipping sparrows, swallows, flickers, flycatchers, chickadees, bald eagles, ravens, and hummingbirds.

From English Camp's main parking area, look for the path in trees at an upper corner of the lot. This leads 0.2 mile to a road crossing and 0.1 mile more to a sign warning of the steeper path ahead. We are dutifully warned that "high heels are not recommended."

Just ahead, at the end of a spur on the right, find the British Cemetery and a plaque commemorating six military men and one civilian who died during the years that the United States–Canada boundary was in dispute. A shooting war did not ensue, and drowning proved to be the greater risk; several succumbed to it.

Continue up the main path another 0.3 mile in moderately steep forest to a junction just before breaking out into the open. Right goes to the first viewpoint. Stroll around the corner to an awesome panorama. Garrison and Westcott Bays are sprawled below, split by English Camp and Bell Point. Two peninsulas obscure Mosquito Pass, the entrance channel, and Haro Strait lies beyond Henry Island. The treeless slopes of Spieden Island, Stuart Island, and B.C.'s Saturna Island are also visible. For the upper viewpoint, return to the last junction and follow the other leg about 0.1 mile to a large rocky meadow and a slightly different perspective from the Olympic Mountains to Mitchell Bay, beyond a stand of garry oak trees. Glacial striations are conspicuous in the exposed bedrock. Be aware that two beaten paths descend from the upper summit, the second just a few yards east of the one you hiked up (the other path leads down the north side of the mountain).

Garrison Bay from Mount Young

SAN JUAN ISLAND—
42. Lime Kiln Point & Deadman Bay

Distance: 0.3 to 2.0 miles round trip

Time: 1 to 2 hours

Elevation gain: minimal to 200 feet

Undoubtedly, the best place to see orcas anywhere in the islands, if not the entire inland sea of Washington, is along the west shore of San Juan Island in the vicinity of Lime Kiln Point State Park. There is no guarantee orcas will be there when you are, but if you visit in late spring or summer and are willing to hang around a few hours, you have about a fifty percent chance of seeing one—if not twenty. In early May 2001, while visiting the state park for this book project, a friend and I had more or less given up on the idea of seeing orcas after an hour of exploring trails and taking notes. After all, it was still before the peak season for sighting orcas and it had been at least a week since they had been observed there. Then suddenly, there they were: two powerful orcas cruising down Haro Strait 300 yards offshore. Within minutes, others followed, including females with young, and the old bull, Ruffles (with the crooked dorsal fin). Ultimately, the entire J pod passed by—20 orcas, including a 4-month-old calf who was pink where the others were white.

Regrettably, the number of orcas in our waters has been declining at an alarming rate, due in part to pollution. For anyone lucky enough to see these remarkable creatures in the wild, it's easy to become inspired to work toward ridding the toxic waste from Puget Sound and the Straits. We humans may find it all very pretty to look at it, but it's a home to orcas. Unfortunately, too few politicians seem willing to tackle clean-up issues in a meaningful way.

Lime Kiln Point is also famous for its historic lighthouse and remnants of the lime kilns and quarries that were once one of the island's major industries. You can find it all at the state park on Westside Road, about 9 miles west of Friday Harbor. From the ferry dock, follow Spring Street then Argyle to Douglas Road; turn left. This road becomes Bailer Hill Road at a curve, then Westside Road when it approaches the coast near the park. The route is well signed.

At the park, walk the barrier-free gravel path down and left 0.1 mile to a viewpoint above the water. Interpretive signs explain the ecology of Haro Strait and why the orcas frequent the area. A scenic path continues north along the rocky shore 0.1 mile to the lighthouse, where one can easily complete a loop to the parking area.

Just above the lighthouse, one can head left at a junction to explore the nearby lime kilns, one of which was recently restored. A path continues past this kiln to several others in various stages of collapse, then switchbacks right just beyond a large old building. The trail follows an old road grade up through the quarry, makes a left turn in the forest, then reaches high ground above for another good view. This quarry was recently acquired by the San Juan County Land Bank which also purchased the area above Deadman Bay immediately south of the park. From the barrier-free trail just before the first orca overlook, head left on a narrow path that runs along the steep bluff (some drop-offs). In about 0.1 mile take a left fork up the hill to bypass a missing trail section on the lower fork. In another 0.1 mile a spur on the left climbs to Westside Road and the parking area, or keep going 100 yards to a steep path down to the beach at Deadman Bay. An old road grade here also climbs to the road above.

Lime Kiln Point Lighthouse

San Juan Island—
43. False Bay

Distance: 0.5 to 3.0 miles round trip

Time: 1 to 2 hours

Elevation gain: none

Note: Check the tide tables before heading out...

What looks like a calm, protected harbor at high tide rapidly transforms with only a modest drop in the tide into a half square mile of mud flats, thus the name, False Bay. Even when the water is up, the pseudo-bay is too shallow for most boats and is generally avoided by astute mariners, with the exception of an occasional canoe or kayak. The bay is a rich microcosm of marine life and has been studied at length. The entire bay and surrounding shores are protected as the University of Washington's False Bay Biological Reserve. Keep that in mind as you visit and treat the place kindly to help ensure continued public access to the area.

To explore the extensive beaches along the bay, leave Friday Harbor on Spring Street, which becomes San Juan Valley Road at the city limits. Turn left 1.6 miles from the ferry dock, and left again on False Bay Road in another 2.5 miles. Park at the turn-out a short mile ahead and clamber a few yards down to the beach. One can ramble right or left along mixed sand and gravel beach below a low bluff. When the water is up, the beach can be narrow, so time the walk with an outgoing tide to avoid bushwhacking on the return. If walking right (west), the upper shore reveals exposed bedrock, enjoyable to walk. A sandy beach between rocky outcrops offers an easy destination 0.5 mile from the start. Beyond this, small trees block the upper beach. One can continue out around a point where the rocky shore steepens (this is more difficult to negotiate as the tide comes up). A mile of similar wandering is feasible along the east shore as well.

San Juan Island—
44. American Camp & Grandma's Cove

Distance: 1.0 to 2.0 miles round trip (or more)

Time: 1 to 2 hours (or more)

Elevation gain: 100 feet

All the hikes at American Camp, the southerly unit of San Juan Island National Historical Park, are enjoyable, and all provide good views of this unique landscape. The walk along the interpretive trail near the park information center can be nicely extended to include a visit to the beach at lovely Grandma's Cove, and to the point nearby that overlooks this cove and the long stretch of beach to the south. For an excellent longer hike, combine this walk with all or part of the 2-mile hike along South Beach (see Hike 45).

From the ferry dock at Friday Harbor, head up Spring Street and angle left on Argyle, then watch for the park sign, turning left on Cattle Point Road. Just past the park entrance sign, 5 miles from Friday Harbor, turn right and park at the information center. Pick up a brochure from the box and walk the interpretive trail through the trees and grounds of the historic camp. The area was occupied by American soldiers 140 years ago to defend the Yankee settlers on San Juan Island from any threat, however unlikely, that might be engineered by the British contingent a few miles to the north. It was

*Grandma's
Cove*

only a mile north of here, in 1859, that American Lyman Cutlar shot a British-owned pig he found rooting in his garden. The incident provoked the standoff regarded famously as the "Pig War," which ultimately placed the San Juan Islands squarely within U.S. territory.

Head right along the white fence, cross the bike path, and continue the guided walk to a grassy path on the right just before the conspicuous flagpole, about 0.2 mile from the start. Follow this gradually downslope another 0.2 mile to the little bay known as Grandma's Cove. Either check out the beach or wander out to the point. In the spring, these open slopes are thick with wildflowers, including prairie starflowers, blue camas, chocolate lilies, chickweed, desert parsley, buttercup, spring gold, shooting stars, blue-eyed mary, native violets, seaside lupine, sheep sorrel, owl clover, and more. Either head back up the same path (the flagpole is a good landmark) and complete the interpretive loop, or continue eastward on a narrow path above the rocky shore. One can walk the latter all the way to the South Beach parking area (about a mile) and beyond.

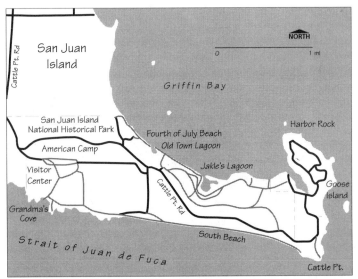

San Juan Island—
45. South Beach & Cattle Point

Distance: 0.5 to 4.0 miles round trip (or more)

Time: 1 to 3 hours (or more)

Elevation gain: minimal

Note: Check the tide tables before heading out...

While visiting American Camp near the south end of San Juan Island, a stroll on the beach is almost mandatory—and South Beach ought to be high on the list of possibilities. More than 2 miles of continuous beach extend from the rocky bluffs at the national historical park's west end almost to the lighthouse at Cattle Point. Walk as little or as much as you like, but if planning on a longer option, time your walk to avoid higher tides. The beach narrows beneath the bluffs as you head farther east. From the park entrance, continue east on the paved road about 1.6 miles and turn right, then left, to the South Beach parking area via Pickett's Lane. To extend the hike westward, see Hike 44.

Meadow behind South Beach, American Camp

Walk left (east) either on the beach or follow the path behind the berm and driftwood line. The backshore area here is broad and full of flowers in spring. The area soon narrows and the bluff rises, which forces the route out onto the beach. On a clear day, the North Cascades' White Horse Mountain and Three Fingers are conspicuous ahead. Mount Rainier is visible to the right. Keep an eye out for orcas—and the whale-watchers pursuing them (they can provide a clue where to look). Where the beach narrows it's important to be aware of a rising tide, since the bluff becomes too steep to climb and your only retreat is back the way you came. The highest tides, of course, are during the new and full moons and during stormy periods. At other times, there is usually enough room to walk. If you have timed the hike correctly, it's possible to saunter all the way to the rocks at Cattle Point. (The Cattle Point Lighthouse can be reached by way of a short path that leaves Cattle Point Road at a sharp curve just before the Cattle Point Interpretive Area. Park at the latter and carefully walk 150 yards back along the road to find the tiny sign marking the footpath.)

SAN JUAN ISLAND—
46. Fourth of July Beach

Distance: 0.5 mile one way (or more)

Time: 1 hour (or more)

Elevation gain: 100 feet

Note: Check the tide tables before you go.

On the north shore of San Juan Island's American Camp, two nearby trailheads provide an opportunity for an easy beachwalk between Fourth of July Beach and Old Town Lagoon, with an option to extend the walk eastward to Jakle's Lagoon and beyond (see Hike 47; *map, p. 136*). The walk offers good views across San Juan Channel to Lopez Island. From the park entrance on Cattle Point Road (see Hike 44 for directions), continue 1.1 miles to the signed trailhead for Fourth of July Beach on the left. Park and walk the short path to the beach (may be impassable during higher tides).

Old Town Lagoon

One can explore northwesterly about 0.2 mile to the national historical park boundary, then head southeast a short distance to Old Town Lagoon, an interesting backwater area that once hosted the island's principal commercial center, such as it was. The town appeared more or less spontaneously after American Camp was established, and catered to the soldiers and settlers of the area for more than a decade. Known as San Juan Town, it earned a reputation for mixing liquor and lawlessness and was eventually abandoned after the boundary dispute was settled and Friday Harbor was selected as the more socially upstanding commercial hub for the island. At the east end of the lagoon, watch for the narrow path leading up through a lush meadow to the Jakle's Lagoon Trailhead above. The path leaves the beach just before the beginning of a steep bank above the beach. The distance from trailhead to trailhead is about 0.5 mile.

SAN JUAN ISLAND—
47. Jakle's Lagoon & Griffin Bay

Distance: 0.9 to 3.2 miles round trip

Time: 1 to 2 hours

Elevation gain: 100 to 300 feet

A good hike to combine with the ridge walk along Mount Finlayson (Hike 48), the trek to Jakle's Lagoon and beyond is almost the only place at American Camp where you can walk in the woods—which says a lot about how wide open the landscape really is on southern San Juan Island. Unfortunately, there is a move afoot to destroy some of the forest and inscribe a serious gash into the side (or top) of Mount Finlayson in order to build a new county road to Cattle Point. The existing road on the south side is, according to the engineers, about to slide into the ocean. Rather than shore it up, the options being seriously considered are to cut a new roadway higher on the ridge or through the forest on the north side—basically where the existing trail is to the lagoons. The impacts to the national park would be extreme, all in the name of the almighty automobile. Some have suggested establishing a small ferry run to serve the Cattle Point residents, while others are insisting on outright purchase of all private lands in that area in order to eliminate the need for a road altogether. Stay tuned. The real controversy is just beginning.

For now, go check out what stands to be lost. A good plan is to hike either to Jakle's Lagoon or Third Lagoon (or both), then turn uphill to meet the Mount Finlayson Trail for the return (or vice-versa). Two connector paths allow for loops of varying lengths. From Friday Harbor, follow the signs to American Camp via Spring Street, Argyle Avenue, and Cattle Point Road. Reach the park entrance and information center about 5 miles from Friday Harbor. Continue southeast another 1.7 miles to the signed trailhead for Jakle's Lagoon on the left (*map, p. 136*).

Head south on the obvious path leading into the forest. Stay left at a junction in 0.3 mile (right is simply an upper trail that runs parallel to the lower one). Continue to a four-way junction just be-

Third Lagoon

yond. Left leads quickly to Jakle's Lagoon, choked with logs, but wild and scenic just the same. A right here would lead across the parallel path on the way to the ridge in 0.1 mile, where a right turn completes a short loop in under a mile. For a more interesting hike, continue straight 0.2 mile to another left turn leading 50 yards to the east side of Jakle's Lagoon; or go straight to another junction with the parallel path above. Keep going straight 0.3 mile to a path on the right that climbs easily to Mount Finlayson for the longer loop option. Just beyond the last lower junction, a short spur on the left leads to Third Lagoon, also worth a look. The lower trail reaches a sign marking the east boundary of the park, although one can continue 0.2 mile more to an inconspicuous trailhead at the end of Cattle Point Road (no parking available). The hike to both lagoons, returning via the ridge, is about 3.2 miles total.

SAN JUAN ISLAND—
48. Mount Finlayson

Distance: 1.8 miles one way

Time: 1 to 2 hours

Elevation gain: 300 feet

The only bad thing about the trail across Mount Finlayson on the south end of San Juan Island is that it isn't long enough. When the day is warm and the flowers brilliant, the ridge walk on Mount Finlayson may be the finest island hike in the State of Washington. Save this gem for a sunny spring or summer day, ideally without a lot of wind. One look at the wind-flagged trees lining the ridge and a glance at the open exposure to the vast Strait of Juan de Fuca, and it's easy to deduce that this can be a very windy place. That said, the hike is still an attractive choice all year long. The views are spectacular. Several loop options exist which can extend the 1.8-mile long ridge route into a 3.2-mile day trip from mountain to sea and back. Most of Finlayson is within the American Camp unit of San Juan Island National Historical Park, and sadly, we could be on the verge of losing it (see Hike 47 for a note on a new county road proposed for the area).

Refer to Hike 47 for directions to the Jakle's Lagoon Trailhead (*map, p. 136*). The Mount Finlayson Trail also begins here (right of Jackle's) and is well marked. One can complete all or part of the 1.8-mile ridge walk and return the same way; arrange for a pick-up at the other end; or leave the ridge at either of two locations and return via the Jakle's Lagoon Trail (see Hike 47). Larger groups could also split up, start at opposite ends, and trade keys (or bikes) in the middle. Find the east end of the trail marked with a tiny sign across the road from a turnout 1.6 miles south of the Jakle's Lagoon Trailhead. Note, however, that the view is slightly better (if that's possible) when walking west to east.

From the Jakle's trailhead, head up the hill, rich with wildflowers in spring (late April to early June is best). Birds and butterflies seem to enjoy the place as much as people do. Quickly reach a kind of plateau with sweeping views out to sea and up and down the

Cattle Point from Mount Finlayson

coast. Oncoming ships make the wide turn into Haro Strait, and pods of whale-watching boats can be seen (and sometimes heard) far below. At a junction barely 0.3 mile from the start, continue straight ahead (a wide grassy path leads left into forest and descends to the Jakle's Lagoon Trail in 0.1 mile).

The main path climbs a short steep section near the road, then for the next mile traces the skyline with awesome unobstructed views all the way to the end. (Another junction offers a second loop option by descending left to Jakle's Lagoon Trail, intersecting the latter near Third Lagoon). A small sign marks the park boundary and the beginning of DNR land. A short spur trail heads right to a slightly different perspective where you can see it all again, and where the lonely lighthouse at Cattle Point pleads for a photograph. Three mountain ranges are visible on a clear day: the Cascades, Olympics, and B.C.'s Coast Range. From the boundary sign it's a quick 0.2-mile descent to the road and turnout noted above.

Shaw Island

San Juan County

A friend remarked once that Shaw Island, the smallest of the ferried islands (7.7 square miles), seems noticeably lacking in public space. Island residents are certainly friendly enough, including the Franciscan nuns who operate the Shaw Island ferry dock, but there is not much to do or see once you arrive. There is a strong sense of isolation here, and some visitors might even feel unwelcome because of it. Quiet roads, littered with "no trespassing" signs, offer a glimpse of the island's lovely waterfront, but there is only one small park with access to a sliver of public beach (described below). Cyclists can explore the island's entire road system in no time, yet roads that seem to approach the more interesting coves, points, and beaches typically end abruptly at fences, dogs, and more signs.

Shaw is popular among small boaters who circumnavigate its rugged shores, yet the perfect little beach at the ferry landing was closed off to kayakers, even those who leave their cars at home. While this kind of isolation—for lack of a better term—is common throughout the islands (some would say throughout America), it may well be that the scarcity of public space, and not the attitude of its residents, is what makes Shaw feel less than inviting. Nevertheless, the island's lonely and obscured beauty can be sampled by either of the two walks listed below. Interestingly, Shaw may have been inhabited by Native Americans more than 9,000 years ago, given the evidence of year-round habitation that was discovered some years ago at Blind Bay.

SHAW ISLAND—
49. Indian Cove & Squaw Bay

Distance: 0.4 to 2.0 miles round trip

Time: 1 to 2 hours

Elevation gain: minimal

NOTE: CHECK THE TIDE TABLES BEFORE HEADING OUT...

South Beach County Park is worth a visit anytime. For a brisk workout, one can walk the two miles from the ferry to the park, or include this short trip as a brief stopover on an inter-island bike outing. A small campground is maintained at the park, but it fills up quickly in good summer weather. From the ferry dock, head up the hill on Blind Bay Road a bit over a mile to Squaw Bay Road; turn left. Look for the park entrance on the left 0.6 mile ahead.

The beach here is excellent, with fine sand and a gentle slope, and views across Indian Cove to Canoe and Lopez Islands. The shallow water warms to swimable temperatures in summer. From the obnoxious private beach sign at the park's east end (see note regarding beach access under the What to Know Before You Go section) one can walk westerly about 0.2 mile to a gravelly beach below

Indian Cove beach

a high eroding bluff. Here, fallen trees make the hiking somewhat cumbersome. Keep a little distance away from the base of the bluff in case something falls from above, and be careful not to get trapped by a high incoming tide. The beach quickly fades to a moderately steep, rocky shore, impassable to most non-rock-climbing mortals.

For a better chance at solitude, walk or ride back to the park entrance off Squaw Bay Road, turn left, then take the second dirt road on the left (close by) which leads to a short path at its end, still within the park. Follow this to a pretty cove on Squaw Bay. Negotiate a little rocky headland to find another beach beyond. Note that the tip of the peninsula between Indian Cove and Squaw Bay is private, though the intertidal area is publicly owned. The walk from the signed park entrance to this beach and back adds about 1.6 miles to the shorter beach walk. In early spring, watch for rafts of bufflehead and red-breasted mergansers, the ever-present kingfisher, and possibly an eagle or osprey feeding in either bay.

SHAW ISLAND—
50. Hoffman Cove

Distance: 0.5 to 2.5 miles round trip

Time: 1 to 3 hours

Elevation gain: minimal

The University of Washington owns and manages a number of biological reserves in the San Juan Islands, some of which are accessible to the public. Others are off-limits to protect sensitive species and ecosystems. These areas not only benefit marine and terrestrial wildlife, they are also used for research, generally in connection with the university's marine lab at Friday Harbor, which unfortunately, is no longer open to the public. The Point George and Hoffman Cove reserve on the southwest shore of Shaw Island is open to passive use only, such as wildlife observation and light hiking. Bikes and dogs are not allowed, nor is hunting, camping, or fires. There is no real parking area, so access by bike is strongly recommended (but leave the bike outside the gate). Note also that use

East of Hoffman Cove

may be further restricted at any time; this is not a park.

To reach the reserve, leave the ferry dock and follow Blind Bay Road about two miles to Hoffman Cove Road; turn left here at the Little Red Schoolhouse. Find the gate on the left about 1.3 mile ahead at the road end. A gravel beach lines the head of the cove. Sign the guest book and follow the grassy road around the field to an old homestead behind madrona trees and a rocky point. The point offers a good view of the rugged Shaw Island coastline, as well as San Juan Island and the Olympic Mountains across San Juan Channel. Turn Island is the nearest point of land across the channel. The small old buildings are for research use and are not open to the public.

From the homestead, briefly follow the path eastward to a gravel beach, a good destination for the shorter 0.5-mile walk. A faint path and rocky scrambling with intermittent gravel beaches lead about a mile farther. The going is generally easy, but can become more difficult in places, especially at higher tides. Turn back when necessary. Note the copious river otter scat, rife with the remains of shellfish, scattered along the shore. After a forested section, a large pasture descends to a split-rail fence above the beach. This makes a good turnaround spot for the longer trek. Beyond, the going gets more difficult as you round the point into Squaw Bay, where a private residence precludes further exploring.

Sinclair Island

Skagit County

One of the lesser-known inhabited islands in the San Juan Group is Skagit County's Sinclair Island, north of Cypress and east of Rosario Strait. In the summer, a handful of permanent residents are joined by many more seasonal islanders in the alleged pursuit of as little as possible. Life at Sinclair is definitely in the slow lane. The island's geography is nothing too dramatic, but since most of the homes are cozied up to the shoreline, what more does one need than a beach and a lounge chair to while away the summer? Other than a small county dock and a few narrow roads, there are no public facilities on the island. There is a small wildlife reserve at the east end and some pleasant walkable beaches on the north and west.

In his book, *Pig War Islands*, David Richardson tells the story of an 1880s opium smuggler, Larry Kelly, who took advantage of the San Juans' proximity to Canada and the multitudinous passages among the islands to further his enterprising nature. Things went so well he was able to purchase a third of Sinclair Island (it was called Cottonwood). He would buy his contraband in Victoria, carefully sail home, then bury the stuff in the beach or on the farm until the right time to sell rolled around. The authorities were onto him early, and while Smuggler Kelly often evaded them or disposed of the evidence overboard, he paid fines and served time on a fairly regular basis, only to devise another clever way to maintain his stubborn livelihood. But more often he found himself outfoxed by the cops, and once jumped from a fast-moving train to avoid arrest. Somehow, he lived to keep his business viable. Repeatedly in and out of jail for decades, Kelly finally gave it up in his seventies and moved to Louisiana. (For more vignettes of life on Sinclair Island, look for a copy of Mary Leach's *Cottonwood Collection*.)

SINCLAIR ISLAND—
51. Sinclair Island Loop

Distance: 2.8 to 4.0 miles loop

Time: 1 to 3 hours

Elevation gain: minimal

NOTE: CHECK THE TIDE TABLES BEFORE HEADING OUT...

Beaches are a mix of public and private tidelands, so don't go where you're not welcome. As with other beachwalks in the islands, enjoy the fresh air, aim for the wild places, and don't disturb anything. That said, one can potentially walk a 3-mile loop via roads and beaches beginning at the county dock on the southwest shore. Walk up the ramp to "Urban" and continue on the dirt road 100 yards to a T intersection; turn right. In 0.5 mile, turn left on another road to North Point; or continue straight 0.6 mile for a pleasant side trip to the 35-acre Sinclair Island Natural Wildlife Area, donated to the public by Mary March Leach before she died in 1989. The overgrown road at the end circles around the orchard to an old house that served as Sinclair's first post office in 1894. Just before the house, a path on the left descends to a gravel-cobble beach.

Back at the last T, head north 0.9 mile to the beach (the last 0.2 mile may be in tall grass); turn left. Walk the beach a mile or so, looking out on Rosario Strait and Orcas Island, and eventually reaching a black, rocky outcrop (no difficulties). This is followed by a few beach homes and cabins including an older summer house known as Viqueen Lodge, maintained by Western Washington University students and staff. Round the point beyond to return to the dock, or look for the road leading back to the intersection above Urban. Roads and paths can be a little confusing here but are manageable nonetheless. The entire loop, including the side trip to the wildlife area, is about 4 miles.

Northwest shore, Sinclair Island

Stuart Island

San Juan County

Stuart Island is about as far to the edge of the San Juans as you can get. A ferry toot farther and you'd be gazing back at the San Juans from Canada. Fortunately, there is no regular ferry service to this 1,786-acre island outpost. Heavily forested, with extensive rocky and rugged shores and little flat ground, development on Stuart has not exploded the way it has on some other islands in the San Juans. There are few roads and few cars (and not much need for them), though two recreational airstrips help generate a modest spike in the summer population. Only the hardiest full-time residents stick it out for the winter. If you can get there safely, Stuart makes a fine destination in the off-season.

For small boaters, getting to Stuart can be a little more of a challenge than some of the other non-ferried islands due to strong currents and tide rips common in the crossing from San Juan Island. The island is a kayaker's favorite, though inexperienced boaters are advised against it. However you arrive, the marine state park sandwiched between Reid and Prevost Harbors is an ideal place for a picnic, perhaps a night's camp above the rocky shore, or just a short hike. But to better appreciate the Stuart Island community and the island's great natural beauty, the moderate hike to the historic Turn Point Light Station is a must.

*Beach at
Prevost Harbor*

STUART ISLAND—
52. Reid & Prevost Harbors

Distance: 0.8- to 2.0-mile loops
Time: 1 to 2 hours
Elevation gain: about 300 feet

The wooded sandstone ridge between Reid and Prevost Harbors forms scenic Stuart Island Marine State Park. The park occupies the narrow neck of a long peninsula and can be accessed from public docks on either harbor. The hike description below begins at Reid, but can be easily adapted to Prevost. If mooring at the docks, information kiosks near both shores will guide you to the two loop trails that meander through the park. The docks themselves are not much more than 200 yards apart and are linked by a broad, easy path. Expect a crowd of boaters in summer.

If starting from the gravel beach and Cascadia Marine Trail campsites at the head of Reid Harbor, look for the path angling left up the steep hillside, climbing 100-plus stairs to the ridge crest. The trail continues along the crest briefly then descends to the Reid dock. Either head left to Prevost and the 1.0-mile northwest loop, or continue up the steep path ahead for the 0.8-mile southeast loop with good views to the south. If taking the latter, as you head over the crest, open madrona–Douglas fir forest on the Reid Harbor side gives way to a more lush Douglas fir–red cedar forest on the Prevost side. A short descent leads to a pleasant stretch just above the rocky shore with views north to Satellite Island and Boundary Pass. The longer 1.0-mile loop skirts a camp area next to a cliff—watch where you park the marshmallow stick—then becomes a bit more gnarly as it climbs in forest to the path that leads back to the steps above the Reid Harbor beach.

Stuart Island—
53. Turn Point Lighthouse

Distance: 5.0 to 5.8 miles round trip

Time: 3 to 5 hours

Elevation gain: about 600 feet

The destination for one of the more pleasant hikes in the San Juans, Turn Point Lighthouse marks the place where Haro Strait meets Boundary Pass, and where ships that miss the turn run aground in another country. The center of these two straits forms the US–Canadian border, and divides the San Juans from the Gulf Islands and Vancouver Island. The quiet road leading to the light station is as placid as a deer trail, with impressive views from the point. The shortest approach is from the beach at the head of Reid Harbor in Stuart Island Marine State Park (see Hike 52), but the hike can almost as easily begin at either of the park's public docks.

From the north end of the beach, look for the easy trail leading past stairs, skirt left of an outhouse, and walk 0.3 mile to a gravel road. Go right and climb steadily for the next 0.6 mile to the historic Stuart Island Schoolhouse, a famous landmark and focus of many

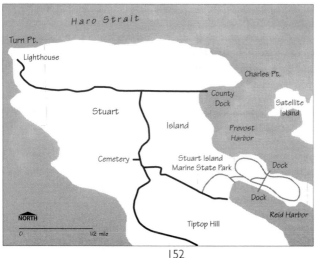

Turn Point

interesting tales (covered well by other writers). Perhaps most interesting is the stamina of the kids who have walked, biked, and boated to and from school for years. Another 0.2 mile beyond the school is a junction, well signed to the lighthouse; head right. Immediately pass a road on the left leading to the island's cemetery nearby, with burials dating from the 1800s.

Continuing on the main road, reach another junction 1.6 miles from the beach; go left. The last leg climbs again, passing an airstrip and a giant blob of conglomerate rock. Just beyond, the drama begins to unfold. Haro Strait is visible through the trees; there's a nice view on the left where the road begins its final 0.2 mile descent to the lighthouse. A second overlook in 150 yards offers sweeping views of the Strait and of Vancouver Island, British Columbia. But use extreme caution here. There is a huge cliff with a slippery edge—sure vertigo for many of us (and no place for kids or pets aloof).

The road meets the light station at an information sign that sums up a little history. Originally built in 1893 and later expanded, the station was manned for 80 years before the mixed miracle of automation displaced the need for humans. Now, beautiful buildings are perched dormant while computers and wireless communications do all the busy work. It seems odd that a charming place like this sits abandoned and boarded up. In any case, you might well have Turn Point to yourself. The view is wide, from south east, 270 degrees worth. There are dangerous cliffs all around, so keep clear of the grassy, sloping edges. Strong tide rips develop just off shore, intensifying the scene. One mid-March afternoon, I watched dozens of Pacific white-sided dolphins feed in the tumultuous water.

Sucia Island

San Juan County

Regarded as one of the most beautiful islands in the San Juans, Sucia Island, north of Orcas, is also one of the busiest during the boating season. The sculpted sandstone shores are a joy to explore, and miles of trails access a number of scenic points, coves, bluffs, and beaches. Sucia's wild charm has made it one of Washington's most popular marine state parks. Literally hundreds of boats may pass by or stop on a single day, so plan to visit midweek, if possible, or in the off-season if you want a better chance to bask in solitude.

Water-motorists, paddlers, and sailors can find their way to Sucia easily enough using other guides and marine charts. Paddlers often launch from North Beach on Orcas Island, but the parking area there is small and generally full in fair summer weather. Bellingham and Lummi Island offer much longer approaches and require a potentially dangerous crossing of Rosario Strait. Check with local sources and paddling guides for other options, and beware of the hazards around Sucia and its neighbors. Less experienced paddlers shouldn't risk the trip without an experienced leader along. Landings and moorages on Sucia are generally at Fossil Bay, Echo Bay, Shallow Bay, and Ewing Cove, all of which provide easy access to campsites, picnic tables, outhouses, and the island's extensive trail system. Two docks and floats are available at Fossil Bay.

The geology of Sucia Island's 564 acres, rich with ancient fossils of marine organisms, has been studied for more than a century. What's known is nicely summarized at a kiosk above the beach between Fox Cove and Fossil Bay. Take a look and find out why the island is shaped like a giant horseshoe. No digging or chipping of fossils is allowed. In 1950, a 1,000 year-old elk antler carving was discovered on Sucia, apparently carved by a Lummi ancestor.

It is hard to believe anyone would consider seriously defacing the island, but at one time Sucia was eyed for a major sandstone quarry and some excavations occurred. Fortunately, the activity was cut short and the island is now protected as a marine state park. Enjoy Sucia, but leave no trace of your visit.

SUCIA ISLAND—
54. Ewing Cove

Distance: 4.6 to 6.6 miles round trip
Time: 3 to 5 hours
Elevation gain: about 200 feet

If sharing a remote island with hundreds of boaters crowding the coves, bays, beaches, and campgrounds of Washington's most popular marine state park is your idea of a serene wilderness getaway, then by all means, head for Sucia Island in midsummer when the sun's out and the seas are calm. This spectacular island gem of verdant forest and sculpted sandstone can attract 100,000 people in a year, most of them, of course, in summer. So why bother? Surprisingly, only a very small percentage of these island-goers will wander more than a couple hundred yards from their beach or boat, leaving miles of relatively lonely trails for the rest of us to enjoy. And there are plenty of quiet places, like on the hike to Ewing Cove, to relax on the rocks and enjoy Northwest living at its finest. Camping is permitted only in designated areas; first come, first served.

As with all the northern outliers, there is no public transporta-

On the trail to Ewing Cove

tion to Sucia. You must sail, motor, or paddle your way to the island; but beware that even the shortest crossing (from Orcas Island) is known for serious currents and exposure to winds and waves. Small boats can land at beaches in protected coves, and larger boats will find floats at Fossil Bay, embraced by the rocky shores of Sucia's southerly arm. Part of Sucia's allure is its giant horseshoe shape, wrapped around Echo Bay and the private Finger Islands. Ewing Cove is at the end of the northerly arm. From the main dock at Fossil, it's a 6.6-mile round trip hike to Ewing Cove. For a shorter 4.6-mile trek, begin at thebeach separating Echo from Shallow Bay.

If starting your hike at Fossil Bay's main dock, walk up the ramp to a kiosk and head right. The trail leads over a hump to a junction;

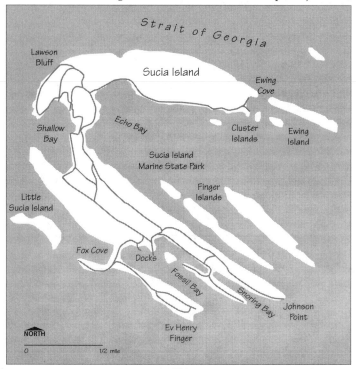

stay left. Walk this flat, narrow service road through mixed forest to another junction 0.5 mile from the dock; head right and right again at the next fork. Go up a hill and head left at the next fork, descending to the head of Echo Bay, 1.0 mile from the start. The wide trail continues past another kiosk (stroll left for a view of Shallow Bay); passes side paths to picnic spots; and rounds a bend to meet the Ewing Cove Trail on the right, 1.2 miles from the Fossil Bay dock. The narrow path is marked by a small signpost just beyond one of the island's many composting and pit toilets—use them.

A short walk in the woods leads to totally scenic sauntering for the next two miles atop the rocky bluff overlooking the bay. You quickly begin to leave the crowds behind and the island is yours, though expect some boats a-buzzing around the bay. That is, unless you are among the minority of enthusiasts who take to the islands in the off-season, in midweek, or during crummier weather.

On a gorgeous late winter Wednesday, I made the entire trek described here and encountered nobody but three folks in a skiff briefly tending their crab pots. Eagles screeched above, kingfishers endlessly squawked and skimmed the water, dozens of harlequin ducks beeped and giggled at my approach, winter wrens cheeped in the brush, a few crows crowed, and the distinct drumming of a pileated woodpecker drifted across Echo Bay. Dark-eyed seals nosed the watery horizon, curiously checking out the land critter. Cormorants, buffleheads, grebes, Canada geese, great blue herons, juncos, and gulls were, like me, soaking up the sunny, 60-degree day.

The trail to Ewing is well maintained, although there are some serious drop-offs that may require keeping the younger kids close by. Madrona, lodgepole pine, Douglas fir, and Rocky Mountain cypress shelter an understory of salal, Oregon grape, wild rose, red-flowering currant, stonecrop, and blue-eyed Mary. Just before Ewing Cove the trail breaks out on an open rocky bench, then beach, with a bit of rock hopping possible when the tide isn't too high. Storm-carved sandstone, off-shore rocks, Ewing Island, and narrow channels enhance the view, you can pick out mainland landmarks like (left to right) White Rock, B.C., Blaine, Sandy Point, Mount Baker, Bellingham, and Lummi Island. If time and energy allow, one can take in Lawson Bluff and Shallow Bay on the return (see Hike 55).

SUCIA ISLAND—
55. Lawson Bluff & Shallow Bay

Distance: 1.6- to 2.8-mile loop

Time: 1 to 2 hours

Elevation gain: about 100 feet

For a small place, Sucia Island offers an impressive variety of natural features and classic Northwest vistas, with trails in all the right places to enjoy them. The short loop along Lawson Bluff and Shallow Bay at the island's west end packs as much scenery per mile as any Island trail, from bizarre rock forms and wide open water, to sea cliffs and a perfectly smooth and sandy beach. For the best lighting make this an afternoon trek.

Begin at the Echo Bay/Shallow Bay kiosk on the service road close to the Echo Bay beach. The shorter loop covers about 1.6 miles; add another mile each way if starting at Fossil Bay (see Hike 54 for directions to both start locations). Walk the narrow road northward, passing the junction with the Ewing Cove Trail on the right to reach

Entering Shallow Bay from Lawson Bluff

another fork 0.2 mile from the kiosk; head right 0.2 mile for the Lawson Bluff Trail (left is a 0.1 mile shortcut to Shallow Bay). Turn right on the well-signed path to Lawson (the wider path curves left and meets the north end of Shallow Bay in 0.3 mile). The trail quickly reaches the bluff and wide open views atop a 100-foot-high vertical rock wall. Patos Island, the northernmost of the San Juan group, lies to the northwest, with the Gulf Islands not far beyond. The trail cuts through a five-foot-thick carpet of rich salal, and in some places runs so close to the edge that a little extra caution is in order.

Generally follow the coastline southwesterly to Shallow Bay, meeting the wide path again in 0.7 mile at a picnic shelter next to the beach. Unless the tide is very high, walk left along this perfect beach toward a high cliff harboring the so-called China Caves—deep holes in the sandstone cliff, well above sea level. A path here leaves the shore and in 0.1 mile reaches another junction. Left goes back to the picnic shelter; head right, up and over the cliffs 0.3 mile to the start at the Echo Bay/Shallow Bay kiosk.

For an extended loop continue along Shallow Bay a short distance to a scenic, less traveled path leading along the south shore. Walk through forest near the shore to a short beach fronting an intriguing stand of dead trees. At the other end of the beach a wide trail leads southeast to another junction; a left here, then a right, and a left again near Echo Bay complete this second 1.2 mile loop.

SUCIA ISLAND—
56. Johnson Point & Snoring Bay

Distance: 2.3 to 5.2 miles round trip

Time: 1.5 to 4 hours

Elevation gain: about 300 feet

If you find yourself at Sucia Island on a busy summer weekend and need a little break from all the people, try the short hike from Fossil Bay to Johnson Point and Snoring Bay. To the 2.3-mile round-trip hike from the dock at Fossil Bay to Johnson Point, add about a mile each way if starting at the Echo Bay/Shallow Bay tombolo. A

Snoring Bay

side trip around Snoring Bay to Wiggins Point adds another 0.5 mile each way. (See Hike 54 for additional information on access to Sucia Island and Fossil Bay; *map, p. 156*.)

From the Fossil Bay dock, walk up the ramp and turn right at the kiosk, then right again on a narrow service road that leads along the beach past a building. The signed junction is just up the hill on the right, 0.2 mile from the dock. Good trail leads through forest and climbs to another junction 0.5 mile farther. Continue straight for Johnson Point; right leads down to Snoring Bay (described below). Views begin just beyond the junction and improve over the next 0.5 mile to the point, with sweeping views of (left to right) the Finger Islands, Georgia Strait, Matia Island, Mount Baker, Lummi Island, Rosario Strait, and Orcas and Waldron Islands. An historic marker and plaque denotes an 1890s survey site. Slippery slabs at Johnson Point and in spots along the trail suggest caution.

Back at the earlier junction, an easy 0.1 mile descent leads to a shore path (stay left) and the tombolo beach for a good look at the steep, parallel rock walls that line Snoring Bay—a great place for a siesta. A muddy, quiet arm of Fossil Bay backs up to the same beach. For the more rugged hike to Wiggins Point, continue across the beach and head uphill on small stone steps to a fork; stay left. Follow the rough path generally near the ridgecrest for about 0.3 mile to a small clearing and a short scramble down the rocks (easy for experienced hikers). The next slabby clearing has good views and makes a good turnaround, since the scrambling becomes more serious beyond this point, with no obvious trail or route. Experienced scramblers can pick their way down thick ledges for the last 0.1 mile without much difficulty, but there are drop-offs, slippery rocks, and a narrow crevasse in the sandstone that's deep enough to get your attention (not a good place for younger kids). Be cautious and remember the way back if you go on.

Back at the tombolo beach, one can explore to the northwest toward Harnden Point, but only scraps of faint trail exist. A few knobs and slabs are perfect for sunning or watching boats venture in and out of Fossil Bay. From the junction north of the tombolo, one can climb back up to the Johnson Point trail or follow the shore, but the latter can be muddy or even underwater at higher tides.

SUCIA ISLAND—
57. Fox Cove & Ev Henry Point
Distance: 1.0 to 2.6 miles round trip

Time: 1 to 2 hours

Elevation gain: 0 to 200 feet

Another wild avenue of Sucia discovery awaits near Fossil Bay where an unusual layout of three scenic beaches lie back to back to back. The convergence includes the sandy beach of Fox Cove sloping northwesterly opposite Fossil's gravelly shore, and a third walkable beach facing southwest toward Orcas and Waldron Islands. A perfect parkland with picnic tables occupies the low upland area between the beaches. No solitude here though, unless you come midweek, or early or late in the season. Expect relative crowds (and crowds of relatives) on nice summer weekends.

Again, starting from the main dock at Fossil Bay, walk northwest to the obvious beach at the head of the bay (*map, p. 156*). If the tide's out, easy beach strolling leftward along this bay, below the narrow peninsula known at Ev Henry Finger, leads to a giant erratic boulder deposited here by the melting continental glacier ice thousands of years ago. The sandy beach on Fox Cove is at least as appealing. "Mushroom Rock" decorates the north shore; and a small peninsula to the south supports a short (0.2 mile) trail along its crest leading to more good views and a barricade just before a cliff.

For the hike along Ev Henry Finger, look for the trail in brush just beyond the lawn area between Fox Cove and Fossil Bay. The trail leads up and over a forested hump then up again to a junction at 0.5 mile. Left or right completes a scenic 0.5 mile loop around the end of the peninsula. A short spur leads to the edge of a cliff at the eastern tip. Drop-offs here and in several other spots suggest caution with kids. Note that there is no easy way to gain the trail anywhere along Ev Henry from the rocky beaches below. If walking the southerly beach, watch for fossils of clams, snails, and ammonites, an ancient octopus relative from the Cretaceous.

Ev Henry Finger, Sucia Island

Turn Island

San Juan County

Only a mile and a half southeast of Friday Harbor, beauteous Turn Island was named by the British to denote the sharp bend in San Juan Channel. Today, Turn receives much attention for its picturesque setting from San Juan Island residents and visitors alike. Turn is also one of only two places in the San Juan Islands National Wildlife Refuge where humans are allowed to visit (the other is Matia; see Hike 28). The island is jointly managed by the U.S. Fish and Wildlife Service and Washington State Parks, so wildlife takes a higher priority here than at most other marine parks. No dock is available. However, there is much to see and do for a morning or afternoon. Rocky shores, sand and pea gravel beaches, mature forest and great views await. A small campground, picnic tables, two composting outhouses, and a 1.5-mile loop trail are provided.

Access to the island is generally via Friday Harbor, although paddlers have the option of a short crossing from a road end immediately west of Turn Island. Currents can run strong enough to be of concern, so the close proximity to San Juan Island should not be taken lightly. For the easier access, follow the road around Turn Point to Pinedrona Road, a narrow lane that leads to a small parking area. There is a 50-yard carry to the beach. Other boaters will often drop by Turn as part of a bigger outing. Two mooring buoys are available off the northwest beach.

Turn Island—
58. Turn Island Marine State Park

Distance: 1.5 mile loop

Time: 1 hour

Elevation gain: minimal

Despite its small size (35 acres), Turn Island is well worth a visit and a stroll just about anytime. A path closely follows the rugged shores and links the beaches and picnic/camping areas at the

Turn Island forest

west end. A good start is at the information kiosk above the northwest beach (see above for access to the island). If the picnic area is busy, cut across the island and head left along the trail above the shore, otherwise simply wander the perimeter of the island left or right. The views change quickly from south (San Juan Channel) to east (Lopez Island) to north (Shaw, Yellow, and Spieden Islands) to west (San Juan). The path is close to the edge in places so due caution is advised for the younger kids. Pass a 12-foot high glacial erratic boulder near the east end. To the west, a small islet can be reached by a beach that emerges at low tide. Note that Turn Island can be subject to a lot of noise from boats, seaplanes, and lawnmowers (and the like) on San Juan Island. It's scenic enough, but it's not exactly pristine wilderness.

Whidbey Island

Island County

Whidbey Island is one of the largest islands in the contiguous U.S., and perhaps the longest, depending on how you measure it. There are at least two other contenders: New York's Long Island and Michigan's Isle Royale—a national park on Lake Superior. At one time, Long Island, a much larger land mass, was declared a peninsula, which could put it out of the running. At 45 miles, Isle Royale is shorter than Whidbey if you measure Whidbey's length by running a meandering course down its sinuous middle. But in total area, Isle Royale's 210 square miles beats Whidbey's 108 square miles. So, what does it all mean? Not much, other than the fact that Whidbey is, by far, the largest island included in this guide. It also accounts for one-fourth of the listings.

The island's early rise, colorful past, and important influence in the early development of Washington State are highlighted in the introduction to this book, and many of the hikes listed explore areas still remembered for their historic significance—Ebey's Landing, Coupeville, the military forts on Admiralty Inlet, the bridge at Deception Pass. But Whidbey's natural environment is also a major draw for those who wish to explore the place on foot. Many miles of bluffs and beaches, four major parks, several stands of old-growth forest, and the dramatic coast of the Deception Pass area are all worthy of a hike.

Despite Whidbey's seemingly rural character along many of its backroads, Island County is one of the most densely populated areas in the state. And that only highlights the need to secure more parks, trails, and preserves before more land gets paved over. Fortunately, island residents have similar concerns and efforts are underway to expand what already exists.

Whidbey Island can be reached by car, bike, or bus via SR 20 and the Deception Pass Bridge on the north end; by frequent ferry service between Mukilteo and Clinton near the island's south end; and by the Keystone–Port Townsend ferry near its middle. Very long shoulder lanes for ferry traffic, up to two miles long, both at Mukilteo and on the island, illustrate how serious the ferry backups can be. If driving, try to avoid the commute hours (eastbound in the mornings, westbound later in the day); on weekends expect bigger traffic lineups heading west Saturday morning and returning east Sunday afternoon. The Mukilteo ferry dock can be quickly reached from I-5 via SR 525 and 526 (well signed). On the island, SR 525 continues up the center of Whidbey for 22 miles before merging into SR 20 near the Keystone ferry terminal. Backroads are generally bike-friendly, and public transit on the island is free!

Whidbey Island—
59. North Beach
Distance: 2.0 to 2.4 miles round trip
Time: 1 to 2 hours
Elevation gain: 200 feet

Clearly one of the best hikes in the Deception Pass Area, North Beach offers excellent views of the high rock walls spanned by the Deception Pass Bridge, as well as the narrow passage below that Captain Vancouver presumed to be a rugged cove in 1792. His chief navigator, Joseph Whidbey, discovered otherwise while reconnoitering the area in a small boat. Tidal currents, sometimes faster than ten knots, can surge through the channel, creating whirlpools and whitewater suggestive of a major river emerging from the mountains. Trails follow the rugged coastline from West Point to the bridge, but there are walkable beaches much of the way as well, which allows for an enjoyable loop with much flexibility.

Parking is limited near the Deception Pass Bridge, so start the hike at the West Beach parking lot below (see Hike 60 for directions and a possible add-on to this hike; *map, p. 170*). At West Beach, park toward the north end (right) and walk right to the rocky outcrop known as West Point. A path bends to the right above the shore (the campground amphitheater is nearby) and soon reaches a point where you can either continue on paths or walk the beach, depending on how high the tide is. Various connecting trails along the way might confuse the route, but just keep working eastward along the shore. Avoid several short, steep boot trails that head over rocks and

Tidal current from Deception Pass Bridge

through the brush by sticking to the much easier path above, or just walking the beach. Several rocky points provide good viewpoints along the way.

At a large beach with a picnic shelter, about 0.7 mile from the start, one can amble right to find a nearby stone and log restroom building next to a parking lot. From the restrooms, walk left (east) a few yards to the corner of the parking lot to find two paths leading into the forest. The one on the left dead-ends at the last beach before Deception Pass Bridge (a worthwhile stroll with an excellent picnic spot), while the trail on the right gradually ascends past large trees to a point where the trail has been carved out of the cliff face, then reaches the south end of the bridge just ahead. New stairs and pedestrian underpasses were recently added beneath both ends of the bridge, which allow for an interesting addition to the hike. One can now climb the stairs to the highway above, follow the walkway to the other end of the bridge, then descend the stairs to pass under the bridge to the other side for the return. The bridge walk adds 0.4 mile to the hike.

WHIDBEY ISLAND—
60. Sand Dune Trail & West Beach

Distance: 0.7 to 2.0 miles (or more) round trip

Time: 1 to 2 hours

Elevation gain: none

Deception Pass State Park is attractive not only for its famous bridge, scenic views, precipitous coastline and old-growth forest uplands, but also for the diversity of landscapes represented here. One of the more unusual places to explore are the sand dunes behind West Beach. Frequent winds off the Juan de Fuca Strait produced the dunes from centuries, if not millennia, of shifting sand particles. The sculpting is impeded where dune grass and other vegetation help secure sand and soil in place, but more barren areas are continually reshaped over time.

A 0.7-mile barrier-free loop trail (paved) winds through the dunes, and much more ambling is feasible along West Beach. To find it, head into the main park entrance off SR 20 across from Cornet Bay Road (about 1.0 mile south of the Deception Pass Bridge), and follow the signs to the enormous West Beach parking area (*map, p. 170*). Walk south (left if facing the beach) to find the paved path near a concessions building. The path splits to form a loop. About 0.1 mile to the left is a wildlife viewing area that overlooks Cranberry Lake and its wetlands—a good birding spot. Either follow the loop around or take a short spur to the beach to wander farther south or return to the start. Aircraft noise from the Whidbey Island Naval Air Station can be a bother at times ("the sound of freedom," as they say), but the beach walk is pleasant and popular in summer. Even on warm days, if planning to wander far, take an extra layer in case the wind picks up.

WHIDBEY ISLAND—
61. Goose Rock & Cornet Bay

Distance: 1.0– to 2.3–mile loops
Time: 1 to 2 hours
Elevation gain: 100 to 400 feet

The trail system at Deception Pass State Park extends across both sides of SR 20. The rocky hill to the east is known as Goose Rock, though its relevance to a goose is something of a mystery. Farther east is Cornet Bay, and beyond that, Hoypus Hill (Hike 62). There are, strangely enough, five different trails linking the Goose Rock area to SR 20 and points west, and several more connecting routes that tie the whole system together. One of the easiest is Discovery Trail, a wide path which more or less makes a straight shot from a trail underpass beneath SR 20 to an Environmental Learning Center (ELC) at Cornet Bay, then returns by way of a similar path higher

Cornet Bay from Goose Rock Perimeter Trail

up the slope. Another path to the ELC leaves SR 20 0.2 mile north of the main park entrance. (The ELC grounds are generally restricted to those involved with the youth programs and activities at the site.) A longer route called the Goose Rock Perimeter Trail begins at the south end of the Deception Pass Bridge where it adjoins the North Beach Trail (Hike 59). The Perimeter Trail generally follows the shoreline east to Cornet Bay then south to connect with the first three trails noted above, as well as with the last of the five, the Goose Rock Summit Trail, which is where the best views are.

The general layout is conducive to two separate loop hikes which can be joined and varied in several ways. Here's one possibility: Start at either the small parking area next to SR 20 at the south end

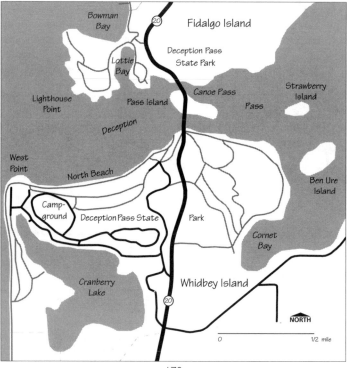

of the Deception Pass Bridge, or at the North Beach parking area for a more scenic alternative. To reach the latter, turn into the main park entrance 1.0 mile south of the bridge and in 0.5 mile stay right for North Beach. Continue 0.6 mile and park to the right of the stone and log restrooms. Three paths converge near the corner of the parking lot. Take the right-hand path which ascends 0.2 mile to the bridge and the stair-steps leading down from the upper parking area. Pass beneath the bridge, then immediately angle right on the Summit Trail (left is the Perimeter Trail—the return route). Stay left at the next junction and right at a fork 100 yards farther (left descends to rejoin the Perimeter Trail). In 0.1 mile more stay left (right joins the Discovery Trail below). Walk another 0.1 mile to the open ridge crest where the views begin. Remember this spot, noting the rounded rock dome to the left.

But first, hike rightward 100 yards for great views (left to right) of the North Cascades, Whidbey Island, Cornet Bay, the Olympics, Cranberry Lake, Juan de Fuca Strait, Lopez Island and the archipelago, Deception Island, Lighthouse Point, and Mount Erie (through the trees). Now head back to the rock dome noted earlier. As you descend the other side, look for the narrow path circling right, immediately below the dome—this is the way down. Moderately steep switchbacks with more good views lead down to an attractive forest of large trees. Meet the well-signed junction with the Perimeter Trail 0.4 mile below the top (just under a mile from North Beach). Head left 1.2 miles to complete the main loop, rising again briefly for another good look at Cornet Bay; stay right at junctions.

To return by way of the Discovery Trail, go right (south) on the Perimeter Trail briefly to an unsigned junction, then either turn right here for the upper leg, or right at the next for the lower leg of the trail. The latter leads to the SR 20 underpass and the North Beach Road just beyond (the parking area is down the hill 0.1 mile). If taking the upper leg of the Discovery Trail walk 0.3 mile to a T junction. Turn left here to meet the lower leg in 100 yards, then turn right to reach the underpass in 0.1 mile. A right at the T climbs to the summit trail. The Discovery Trail loop, if beginning at the North Beach parking area, is about 1.0 mile round trip.

WHIDBEY ISLAND—
62. Hoypus Hill

Distance: 2.0 to 3.2 miles round trip
Time: 1 to 2 hours
Elevation gain: 100 to 300 feet

Deception Pass State Park is well known for it trails and beach walks along miles of spectacular coastline, but perhaps less known for its old-growth forests. Visitors exploring the North Beach Trail (Hike 59), and even those driving to the North Beach parking area can get a good look at this impressive forest, including Douglas firs more than six feet in diameter. Similar forest lies to the east of Cornet Bay in a much less known outlier of the park called Hoypus Hill. An easy hike leads through a mile of old forest and big trees, with the possibility of extending the hike into younger forests and along the beach nearby. A 3.2-mile loop is also feasible.

To find the trail, turn east off SR 20 onto Cornet Bay Road, immediately across from the main park entrance. The road soon reaches the bay, then a picnic area and boat ramp in 1.5 miles. Just beyond is a good view of both Deception Pass Bridges. At 2.2 miles, park on the right at an old quarry. (The road ends 0.3 mile farther at Hoypus Point where there is easy access to the beach.)

The trail begins close to the road and angles left past a gate. Ascending gradually, the wide path is in generally good condition, although it is not as well maintained as trails in other areas of the park. In less than 0.2 mile, watch for a narrower path on the right that is a possible return route for the 3.2-mile loop. This trail may appear a little rough at the start, but it improves quickly. However, there may be a short brushy section (with nettles) and fallen trees to clamber over, depending on when the trail was last maintained. For now, continue straight on the main path as you begin to see larger trees, and a huge, recently broken-off snag at 0.4 mile. The next 0.5 mile is a superb forest walk, passing many Douglas firs in the range of five to seven feet across and at least one large Sitka spruce among a grove of cedars. At 0.9 mile the path steepens and homes become visible to the left. At 1.0 mile a break in the trees gives a good view (near a house) of Ala Spit and Hope Island below, and peaks of the North Cascades beyond. This makes a good turn-around point for a 2.0-mile round trip through the old growth.

To continue the loop hike, keep going another 0.2 mile to a logging road; stay right. After a short, steep section continue straight and down slightly on a grassy path (a rough logging grade curves left). From here, mostly downhill walking leads to an inconspicuous path on the right, about 1.0 mile beyond the viewpoint. The path may be somewhat overgrown as it leads through an area of stinging nettles (long pants, nippers, or a stick can help keep them at bay). If you come to a steep, well-used path on the left you've missed the turn, and need to backtrack about 0.2 mile. The possibly overgrown trail improves after 0.1 mile and is easy going for another 0.6 mile to a T. Turn right to complete the loop in 0.3 mile. A left here on the main path leads quickly back to the trailhead. For more easy walking and good views, head to the road end and walk the beach out around Hoypus Point (assuming the tide is out).

*Hoypus Hill
old growth*

Whidbey Island—
63. Ala Spit
Distance: 1.0 mile
Time: 1 hour
Elevation gain: none

A simple beach walk, short and scenic, awaits at Ala Spit on the northeast end of Whidbey Island and at the northern reach of Skagit Bay. The site was acquired by Island County in 1994 and includes about 1 mile of public beach, the 8-acre spit, and 4 acres of uplands. Paddlers will find a Cascadia Marine Trail campsite at the southeast end. To get to the spit, leave SR 20 at milepost 39.8 and head east on Troxell Road for 4 miles. Angle left on Geck Road just after rounding a bend (the turn is easy to miss). Park at the bottom of the hill.

The walk needs no real description. Simply walk the path along the berm, or walk the fine gravel beach on the right. The left side can be mucky but turns to sand farther out on Ala Spit. Bountiful driftwood will occupy the kids, while great views entertain the rest of us. White Horse Mountain and Three Fingers are conspicuous on the horizon to the right, with Skagit Island and Mount Erie to the left. Mount Baker rises to the northeast beyond nearby Hope Island. Skagit and Hope Islands are within Deception Pass State Park, but there are no facilities on either island and camping is not allowed. Should you be tempted to visit, keep in mind that very strong currents run through these passages. From the spit in June 2001, I watched an osprey snag a fish fifty yards offshore.

Ala Spit

64. Ponteio Beach & Rocky Point

Distance: 0.5 to 3.0 miles round trip

Time: 1 to 2 hours

Elevation gain: none

NOTE: CHECK THE TIDE TABLES BEFORE HEADING OUT...

The name of Ship's Master and island finder, Joseph Whidbey, now immortalized in the name of one of the contiguous United States' largest islands, has also been given to a small state park on the island's northwest shore near Oak Harbor. Master Whidbey was apparently the first European visitor to get his rowboat stuck in the mud at Penn Cove, while he and his companions were also the first whites to introduce themselves to the Skagit natives already living on the island. Captain Vancouver named the island in his honor after Whidbey discovered that this substantial land mass was not, as had been presumed, a peninsula. The narrow channel Mr. Whidbey navigated was thus named Deception Pass.

It is fitting to have a park named after someone so prominent in the region's history, even if the park is somewhat limited in its offerings to the public. For dramatic scenery and a closer look at Whidbey's principal discovery, head for Deception Pass State Park a few miles to the north (see Hikes 18, 19, and 59). Joseph Whidbey State Park, on the other hand, is a fairly tame place, good for a picnic, a view, and a beach walk. A maze of boot trails in adjacent forest hold potential, but hints of informal transient use (in spring of 2001) suggest the area may not be well monitored. Maybe stick to the beach area for now. Military aircraft buzz this part of the island often, so expect some screaming decibels now and then. Also, training exercises in the area may involve the use of live ammunition— obviously a good time to avoid the place (a red flag on a pole indicates live firing may be underway). Nevertheless, the beach is usually open and walkable. An interesting backshore of extensive wetlands skirted by a path makes the area worth an occasional visit.

From the traffic light in Oak Harbor where SR 20 turns west (at the intersection with Pioneer Way) follow the highway to where it curves left and turn right on Swantown Avenue. Continue 3 miles to a stop sign; the park entrance is straight ahead. Picnic tables on the hill offer a huge view into the wild blue of Juan de Fuca Strait and the waters sailed by Whidbey and Vancouver barely two centuries ago. Amble down to the beach and either walk it or the path behind the driftwood. The public beach and trail extend south a short distance to homes and a second small beach access next to the road. Most of the public shore is to the north, toward Rocky Point 1.5 miles distant. The point itself is small but the rocks are beauteous. Just before the point is the Rocky Point Picnic Area, intended more for military personnel, their families and guests, but open to the public. A large backwater marsh area may be of interest to birders. Because of the proximity of the Navy base, access may be restricted at times. Do not head inland from the beach area.

WHIDBEY ISLAND—
65. Monroe Landing & Blower's Bluff
Distance: 0.5 to 3.4 miles (or more)

Time: 1 to 2 hours (or more)

Elevation gain: none

NOTE: CHECK THE TIDE TABLES BEFORE HEADING OUT...

Perhaps the best beach walk on the east shore of Whidbey Island this a 2-mile stretch around Blower's Bluff begins on the north side of Penn Cove and curves northward toward Oak Harbor. The public tidelands extend nearly 5 miles, essentially from Monroe Landing north of Coupeville all the way to City Beach Park. The northerly portion tends to be much more civilized, while the stretch below the bluff has a feeling of remote wildness that inspires one to imagine what life might have been like here two centuries ago. It was spring 1792 when Ship's Master Joseph Whidbey sailed into the cove, finding the area already inhabited by an amiable, industrious and culturally advanced society of Native Americans. In fact, the Skagit Tribe had been living in permanent villages on Penn Cove at least 500 years before Whidbey's "discovery." The area is now

*Klootchman Rock below
Blowers Bluff*

within the Ebey's
Landing National Historical Reserve.

Begin the walk at
the Island County
beach access at the junction of Penn Cove and Monroe Landing
Roads. Find the latter off SR 20 at milepost 29.2 and head south 1.7
miles to the beach. Check out the interpretive signs, then walk eastward (left) on an excellent sandy beach fronting a marshy area behind the driftwood. Downtown Coupeville and the red wharf are
conspicuous across Penn Cove. As you leave the homes behind, the
bluff rises considerably and the beach becomes gravelly, with the
coarser rocks encrusted with copious barnacles and mussels. Muddy
or sloppy sand in the flats can act almost like quicksand, so the best
bet is to stay high on the beach for most of the walk. However, it's
also good practice to keep some distance from the toe of the bluff in
case something decides to break loose. Use good judgement. At one
point a spring flows like a small waterfall down the green face of
the bluff, where spreading garry oak trees lean out over the rim 200
feet above.

Pass several glacial erratics, including a very large boulder, flat
as a picnic table. As you round the point, Mount Baker comes into
view, as well as the entrance to Oak Harbor and Crescent Harbor
beyond. The beach becomes cobbly with many small boulders, but
is still quite passable. At about 1.7 miles, reach an enormous, zebra-
striped boulder known as Klootchman Rock (Chinook jargon for
"woman"), surrounded by large fragments and looking as anomalous as an eighteenth-century sailing ship. The bluff continues
around the next bend, but the shore becomes inhabited again, then
more so as you approach Oak Harbor. Klootchman Rock makes a
good destination and turnaround point for a 3.4-mile walk.

Whidbey Island—
66. West Beach South

Distance: 0.5 to 6.0 miles round trip

Time: 1 to 4 hours

Elevation gain: none or minimal

Note: Check the tide tables before heading out...

Whidbey Island may be famous for the big bridge and scenic rocky shores at its north end (Deception Pass), but there are many miles of wild coastline, particularly on the west shore of the island, that are equally appealing to explore on foot. High eroding bluffs, sometimes rising several hundred feet above the beach, provide a great setting for aimless and bountiful beach rambling. The extensive bluff along West Beach, southwest of Oak Harbor, is one of the more scenic and accessible areas to visit. Some tidelands are private, though public access has been allowed, so please respect the courtesy and privacy of adjoining residents and do nothing that may offend them. Enjoy the walk—as they do—and move on. (*Check the tide tables, and see the note on beach access on p. 49.*)

In its entirety, West Beach spans about 14 miles, most of it public, from Deception Pass State Park south to Point Partridge within Fort Ebey State Park. The walk described here covers the southerly 3 miles, from the Hastie Lake Road beach access to Point Partridge. Normally, one can also access the bluff walk at Libbey Beach Park, 0.5 mile north of the point, although this access was still temporarily closed in spring 2001 for storm damage repair. Access to points north of Hastie can be more problematic. For the 3-mile walk (or less), begin either at Fort Ebey State Park or Hastie Lake Road. See Hike 67 for directions to Fort Ebey and details for continuing the walk farther south. To reach the Hastie Lake access, follow SR 20 south of Oak Harbor to about milepost 28.4 and turn west onto Hastie Lake Road. Continue 2.5 miles to West Beach Road to find the large parking area directly ahead. Note the beach-goer rules on a sign near the boat ramp, then saunter left (south) past a couple of houses.

As you leave civilization behind, the bluff immediately begins to rise, topping 200 feet within the first half-mile. Suddenly, it's as if

West Beach, south of Hastie Lake Road

you're walking in a gorge with one wall missing. As always, be extra cautious when walking below steep, eroding bluffs. A few small slides are also evident, so stay back from the base in case something decides to let loose without warning. Avoid the area altogether during higher tides when waves churn the upper beach (note the dearth of driftwood). The high bluff is sculpted in a variety of forms, particularly where small drainages empty over the brink. Wildflowers cling to breaks in the wall, while both marine and terrestrial birds seem to flourish here. Species observed on a recent spring hike included oystercatchers, pigeon guillemot, harlequin, cormorant, loon, bald eagle, American goldfinch, redtail hawk, swallows, crows, gulls, and oddly enough, a mourning dove.

The bluff diminishes after about 2 miles. At 2.5 miles, a log-piling bulkhead along the shore roughly marks the Libbey Beach access. From there, round a gradual point to the broken remnants of a Fort Ebey gun battery as you enter Fort Ebey State Park. Just ahead, climb a short set of steps and path leading to a bluff-top view, picnic tables, and restrooms. Boulder-strewn Point Partridge is close by, 0.5 mile from Libbey Beach. Whether you walk to the point or not, allow enough time to avoid a high tide on the return.

WHIDBEY ISLAND—
67. Point Partridge Beach & Bluff

Distance: 0.3 to 3.5 mile loops

Time: 1 to 3 hours

Elevation gain: 100 to 300 feet

NOTE: CHECK THE TIDE TABLES BEFORE HEADING OUT...

Fort Ebey is one of a trio of military sites that were developed in the first half of the twentieth century to defend America from any foe attempting an approach via Admiralty Inlet, the principal marine passage into the Puget Sound region. Fort Casey nearby, and Fort Worden, at Port Townsend, were developed much earlier and remained on alert during the First World War. Fort Ebey was developed in response to the potential Japanese threat to the mainland during WWII. However, none of the three ever fired a shot at an enemy target, and all three sites have long since been decommissioned and converted to historic parks. In 1990, 416 acres of adjacent DNR land were added to the park. Fort Ebey and Fort Casey, conveniently sited at either end of Ebey's Landing National Historical Reserve, also happen to offer some of the best beach and bluff walks in the Puget Sound region. To extend the Point Partridge beach walk described here to Fort Casey farther south, see Hike 74.

From SR 20 milepost 25.4, turn west on Libbey Road, then take a left in 0.9 mile on Hill Valley Drive. In 0.7 mile head right to pass the information center and right again to reach the parking lot and picnic area in 0.5 mile at the road end near Lake Pondilla (*map, p. 182*). Either head left of the restrooms and up briefly to the bluff trail among prime picnic sites, or right of the restrooms and follow the path about 100 yards down to the lake. Lake Pondilla is surrounded by hillsides, indicative of its location inside a "kettle" (see Hike 70 for an explanation), while Sitka spruce trees may hint at a microclimate like that on the west coast of Vancouver Island. Wander left above the shore to return to the bluff at a junction with the earlier route. Enjoy the view and either head left along the bluff or descend easily to the beach, returning later by way of the bluff, as described here.

Partridge Point from near Perego's Lagoon

From the beach, one could walk right all the way to Hastie Lake Road beneath high eroding bluffs (see Hike 66), but for this walk head left past the bermed beach where a backwater area is clogged with logs. For a very short loop at the other end of this berm take the path which ascends easily to the small parking area you passed coming in. Head left and up through trees to regain the top of the bluff and the main parking area. For the longer hike, continue past the end of the berm and immediately round Point Partridge where the wave-thrashed upper beach is covered with small boulders the size of bowling balls and larger, and is more easily walked at lower tides. This is the westernmost point of Whidbey Island and marks the entrance to Admiralty Inlet. The bluffs rise again over the next mile, always scenic, though not so smooth and green as the bluff above Perego's Lagoon two miles to the south. About 0.7 mile south of the point, rough paths lead up a weakness in the lower bluff to the Fort Ebey gun battery and the bluff trail. Or continue another 0.7 mile to a wide, easy trail angling up the higher bluff.

Once atop the latter, stay left on the main path, passing several

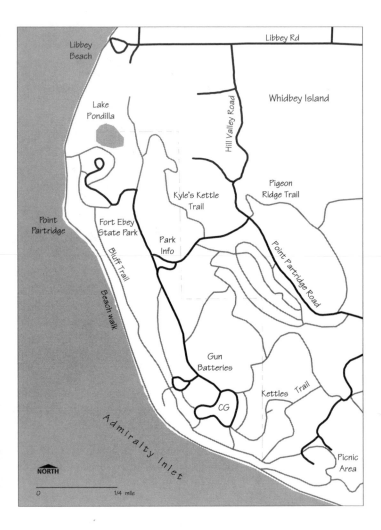

picnic sites before emerging at a parking area at the end of Point Partridge Road, about 0.4 mile from the beach. Continue left on the path to where it crosses another road and revisits the top of the bluff just beyond a group campsite. The next stretch is a joy to walk, with good views amid fragrant wild roses and wind-blasted trees. Pass several junctions leading right to the Kettles Trail (see Hike 68) and the Fort Ebey campground before reaching the gun battery and another wide open vista where a sprawling meadow demands at least a short break (a flashlight is helpful to explore the bunker). The last stretch of bluff trail tends to stay behind a thick hedge of salal, wild rose, snowberry and other shrubs and trees that obscure the view most of the way back to the start. Stay left at a junction, pass another gun placement and the Point Partridge Beacon (don't linger, the horn is extremely loud), before reaching the small parking area 100 yards before the finish.

WHIDBEY ISLAND—
68. Kettles Trail
Distance: 2.2 to 3.9 miles one-way
Time: 1 to 2 hours
Elevation gain: 200 to 400 feet

Extending almost 4 miles from Fort Ebey State Park to Coupeville, the Kettles Trail provides a significant regional link for nonmotorized transportation, and most of it may be of more interest generally to cyclists than hikers. The easterly 2 miles is paved and runs parallel to SR 20, while the westerly 0.5 mile traverses a dark thicket of uninteresting forest. That leaves about 1.2 miles of more interesting and walkable path that could easily be combined with other hikes in the area which explore the unique geology of the Kettle Lands (see Hikes 69 and 70).

To walk the westerly 1.7-mile portion, head for Fort Ebey State Park by turning west off SR 20 at milepost 25.4, then go left in 0.9 mile on Hill Valley Drive. Follow this winding road 0.7 mile to where a sign points right to the information station and campground. Instead continue straight ahead to a trailhead at the end of this road.

Instead of following the sign to the beach, walk right on a path through forest that leads shortly to a road crossing (access to a group campsite) and the edge of the bluff 100 yards beyond. Enjoy the bluff views, pass the Hokey-Ka-Dodo Trail, and take the next right to the campground, passing several walk-in sites.

Where you meet the campground road make an immediate right on the Kettles Trail. Stay right at the first junction, left at the next, descend a long hill, and continue straight to another junction where one more right reaches the road leading to the trailhead. Walk down the road a few paces to find the Kettles Trail, 1.0 mile from the start. Stay right at the top of a short hill then take another right and follow this wide, easy path through interesting salal, rhododendron and Douglas-fir forest. Meet the paved path above SR 20, 1.2 miles from the last paved road.

One can continue walking all the way to the Main Street overpass at Coupeville, with good views of Ebey's Prairie, or for a possible long loop via roads, bluff, and beach back to the park, first make sure the tide there is not too high, then walk 1.4 miles of paved path to Sherman Road. Turn right (use caution along this road section), then right again in 0.3 mile onto Cemetery Road to pick up the trail leading out to the bluff. See Hikes 71 and 72 for the bluff and beach return to Fort Ebey and the trail leading back up the bluff to the starting point for this hike.

WHIDBEY ISLAND—

69. Pigeon Ridge/Raider Creek Loop

Distance: 1.3-mile loop (or more)

Time: 1 hour

Elevation gain: 300 feet

For an easy introduction to the unusual geography of the Kettle Lands at Fort Ebey State Park, try the 1.3-mile loop combining Pigeon Ridge Trail with parts of the Raider Creek, Shepard's Crook, and Princess Run Trails (see Hike 70 for an explanation of the kettle formations and a longer loop hike). With nearly 30 miles of hiking, mountain biking, and equestrian trails waggling through the Kettle

Rhododendrons blooming on Pigeon Ridge

Lands, there are obviously many other ways to explore the area and far longer options to consider. Begin the loop at one of two small turnouts just past the gate for the road leading to the Point Partridge Trailhead. The trail begins at the gate and is well marked (this gate is at the intersection of the Point Partridge Road and the road leading to the park information center; *map, p. 182*).

Head up the hill winding through forest to a junction with the Fisher Ridge Trail on the left at 0.3 mile. But stay right and continue 0.3 mile more to cross the Point Partridge Road, ambling left briefly to find the Raider Creek Trail on the right. Follow this 0.1 mile to a junction with the Campground Trail (an alternative approach for those staying at the park). Instead, turn right just ahead on Shepard's Crook Trail and stay left at a fork in 30 yards. This trail gradually descends into one of the kettle formations, then switchbacks more steeply to the kettle bottom, not quite a mile from the gate. The trail immediately climbs back up a low ridge, descends once more into another forested pit, then climbs to meet the Princess Run Trail. Raider Creek Trail is close by on the left, but head right 0.1 mile and then left briefly to reach the road near the starting point.

WHIDBEY ISLAND—
70. Ebey Kettle Lands

Distance: 2.0 to 5.3 mile loops (or more)

Time: 1 to 3 hours

Elevation gain: 200 to 600 feet

Immediately east of Fort Ebey, near the center of Whidbey Island, the retreating Vashon Glacier left behind some impressive evidence of its passing—a scattering of giant depressions separated by narrow ridges, all of which is now heavily forested. Now a recognized geological site within the Ebey's Landing National Historical Reserve, the history of the kettles goes back thousands of years when orphaned chunks of glacier ice were buried in the glacier's rocky outwash. The icebergs melted, leaving voids in their place which were so large—sometimes more than a 200 feet deep—that they have yet to be filled by the intervening years of erosion. If the land was unforested, the drama would be perhaps more striking, but it is still a treat to wander in and around these odd forested forms, imagining a vast icy landscape giving way to the forces of a warming planet.

This hilly terrain has also charmed the mountain biking community into building numerous trails into nearly every cranny and nook of the kettles. Some trails are open to horses too, so be warned, this is not strictly a hiker haven, but worth a visit nonetheless. To avoid the bikes, try a weekday, ideally in May when wild rhododendrons are blooming everywhere. A map of the area is posted at several information kiosks and many of the trails are signed at intersections, although a carry-along map is extremely helpful for first-time visitors (try www.traxmaps.com for more information; *see also map on p. 182*). Many loops of varying length are feasible, but if a little direction is helpful, try the following 5.3-mile loop as an introduction to the area. Note that new trails are still emerging, so minor adjustments may be necessary.

From the Fort Ebey Picnic Area (see Hike 67 for directions), follow the bluff trail south past the Point Partridge Beacon and go left at the fork; head right on the road briefly then left on a wide path (0.3 mile to here). In 200 yards, turn right on Kyle's Kettle Trail and stay right just ahead. This scenic path winds around and down into a kettle full of Douglas fir and thick rhododendrons. Climb back up and meet the park entrance road a mile from the start (the Pigeon Ridge Trail is close by to the left—see Hike 69). Jog right then left onto Raider Creek Trail for 200 yards, continue straight, then stay right at the next junction just ahead and straight again at the next, finally reaching Point Partridge Road 0.6 mile from the last road. (One can short-cut the next section by walking this road right 0.3 mile to the kiosk at Cedar Hollow—see below.)

To continue, walk the road right briefly, then go left on Mainline Trail, crossing under powerlines. Ignore the next two lefts but take the third for Hugh's Delight. Swing right at a junction then straight at the next, soon descending back to the Mainline, 0.7 mile from the last road crossing. Stay left, pass another fork, then go right at a T onto Fern Grove Trail (SR 20 is audible nearby); stay right, then at the next junction (Bakerview Trail on left) take an inconspicuous path on the right called DP Cutoff. Then turn left up the hill to begin the High Traverse, a short, pretty stretch along a narrow ridge above another large kettle. Pass two more junctions (staying right) to find the Kettles Trail, a wide gravel path leading right, then straight, to the powerlines. Left here returns to Point Partridge Road at an information kiosk, about 3.7 miles total from the start. One could turn left here on Cedar Hollow to reach a nice section of the bluff trail (see Hike 67), or walk up the hill to find the Kettles Trail leading to the campground. Pass through the latter to the gun battery on the left and walk the bluff trail rightward back to the starting point (1.6 miles from the Cedar Hollow kiosk)—or just keep exploring the kettleland maze. If you end up lost or confused, remember that the powerlines generally run north-south through the kettles, the bluff and Point Partridge Road are to the west, and noisy SR 20 is to the east. If you're out later in the day, be sure to bring a flashlight just in case.

WHIDBEY ISLAND—
71. Ebey's Prairie
Distance: 2.0 miles (or more) round trip
Time: 1 to 2 hours
Elevation gain: 100 feet

In 1850, a young lawyer-pioneer who would become one of the more illustrious figures in the history of Washington State staked a claim amid a large natural prairie almost at the center of Whidbey Island. Isaac Ebey's perfect homestead overlooked Admiralty Inlet and the Olympic Peninsula. The fertile ground promised a life of prosperous farming in a lovely setting. Before moving to the island from Elliott Bay, Ebey had already achieved a certain notoriety for, among other things, the naming of Olympia, the future state capitol, and the "discovery" of Lake Washington (he called it Geneva). He also served as the Oregon Territorial Representative for most of western Washington when it was still one giant county.

But Isaac Ebey met a tragic end after just seven years on the

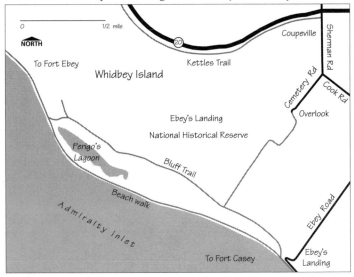

Ebey's Prairie and Landing

island. A bloody ambush near Port Gamble by the U.S. Steamer Massachusetts had taken the lives of 27 Haida Indians, including a chief. To avenge the attack, the Haidas identified Ebey as a white "chief," and on a midsummer evening in 1857, they killed him, left his body, but not his head (eventually the body parts were reunited). Today, you can visit the historic cemetery where many of Whidbey's early settlers were buried, and look across the ancient lakebed that is Ebey's Prairie.

From SR 20, just west of Coupeville, turn south on Sherman Road, then stay right in 0.3 mile to find the cemetery and Ebey Prairie Overlook just ahead. An easy, mile-long path leads from here to a spectacular viewpoint on the bluff above the beach. The path drops slightly to a gravel road, follows the shoulder (well signed) then a fence line to the scenic bluff. To reach the beach, walk another 0.3 mile left (see Hike 72 for the complete loop along the bluff past Perego's Lagoon and back via the beach). If wandering the cemetery, look for a good piece of prose at the Davis blockhouse, one of many such structures built in the mid-1800s to provide refuge in the event of an attack by Indians.

WHIDBEY ISLAND—
72. Perego's Lagoon & Bluff
Distance: 3.5 miles round trip
Time: 1 to 3 hours
Elevation gain: 250 feet

Clearly one of the finest hikes on Whidbey Island, this 3.5-mile loop takes in the high bluff northwest of Ebey's Landing, and returns by way Perego's Lagoon and the beach, and can easily be extended by several miles with more beach wandering to the north or south. There are countless places to linger or enjoy lunch in the sun or shade, and the views are virtually non-stop from start to finish. From SR 20 at the Main Street pedestrian overpass in Coupeville, turn south and follow Engle Road about 1.7 miles to Hill Road. Turn right and follow this scenic road to the beachfront trailhead at Ebey's Landing (*map, p. 188*).

From the parking area, climb the steps and path to the top of the low bluff and head left, climbing gradually to a junction. The

Perego's Lagoon and Bluff

trail on the right leads along a fence line to a cemetery (see Hike 71). Continue up the bluff to improving views. The perfectly smooth path negotiates minor ups and downs and hugs the edge for more than a mile. Windswept Douglas fir trees line the right side of the path, and the sweeping steep bluff falls away to the left. From high above Perego's Lagoon, Port Townsend, Protection Island, and the Olympics are visible across Admiralty Inlet. Fort Casey and Admiralty Point are to the left, four miles away. Large freighters and other ships ply the Inlet, while their breakers stir the beach below.

At the far end of the bluff, find a junction; right goes a few yards to one more good sitting spot, but head left to descend steeply for about 200 yards to the beach. To the north (right), the bluff sweeps above Point Partridge Beach. Look carefully and you may be able to discern the stairs and path descending the bluff from Fort Ebey State Park a mile away. For the return to Ebey's Landing, though, head left (southeast) and either walk the beach or a path behind the driftwood. The brackish lake, Perego's Lagoon, is named for an early settler on the adjacent upland. From the north end of the lake, allow an hour for the 1.7-mile walk back to the landing.

WHIDBEY ISLAND—
73. Historic Coupeville
Distance: 0.5 to 1.7 miles round trip
Time: 1 to 2 hours
Elevation gain: minimal

Named for Thomas Coupe, the sea captain who laid out the original town in the early 1850s, Coupeville is not only the seat of Island County government, it's a fine place for a stroll through history. Stop by the small, but outstanding museum near the red wharf downtown for an introduction to the history of Coupeville, nearby Ebey's Landing, and Whidbey Island in general. Then pick up a brochure and map for an historic walking tour of the city. (The museum is generally open Friday through Monday most of the year, and every day in summer.) A second walking-tour map can be found

Coupeville Wharf

at the information kiosk near the wharf, or simply amble along more or less as described below.

First walk out to end of the wharf at the west end of Front Street to where the bones of Rosie the grey whale are nicely displayed—a community project that has become quite an attraction. Return to Front Street, then follow the walkway around the 1897 livery stable (now several shops). Next walk eastward a few blocks to see a number of buildings dating back to 1864—among the oldest standing structures in Washington. Turn back anytime, or continue along the gravel path to a sharp curve; turn left on 9th Street to find Captain Coupe's little house and barn on the left, built in 1854 (0.6 mile from the wharf). Back at the museum, Indian racing canoes and the Alexander blockhouse, built in 1855, are worth a look. Also, find an herb garden out front, and a drought-tolerant flower garden just up the path off the end of Front Street (find more information on both inside the museum). Follow the path up the hill to the Town Park and another path on the right leading down to the beach. If the tide is out, one can walk the beach back to the wharf where a narrow stairway leads up to the starting point.

WHIDBEY ISLAND—
74. Fort Casey & Admiralty Point
Distance: 0.5 to 6.0 miles round trip (or more)
Time: 1 to 4 hours (or more)
Elevation gain: minimal

Fort Casey, originally developed around 1900 as a powerful military defense installation, is now a popular state park offering access to miles of public beach and short trails along a scenic bluff. The grounds include gun batteries, concrete bunkers, assorted relics, and an historic lighthouse. Fortunately, the large-caliber guns mounted on the bluff at Fort Casey were never fired at an enemy target. A maze of underground corridors, walkways, and crow's nests are partly open to easy exploring, but some areas are unlit and windowless (a flashlight is helpful). Wander the scenic bluff, or a beach that extends to Ebey's Landing and beyond (up to 8 miles).

From SR 20 at Coupeville's Main Street, turn south at the pedestrian overpass, following Engle Road about 3.5 miles to the signed park entrance on the right (just before the Keystone Ferry terminal). Head up the hill past the campground turnoff and picnic area, and park next to the huge lawn in front of the compound. Either head straight for it, or wander well to the left to find a path leading up to several buildings with green roofs, 3-inch pedestal guns, and more bunkers. Head right (west) past these structures to the more sprawling mass of gun mounts near the point. Corridors and narrow stairways lead everywhere—a fun place for kids to roam, but beware of serious drop-offs above lack protective railings (adding railings would deface the historic value of these facilities).

At some point, walk to the south end of the gun batteries to find a grassy path and steps leading down to the beach. Unless the tide is high, one can walk the beach northward (or the wide mowed paths above) to another set of steps leading up the low bluff. From here, another 0.2 mile of grassy path leads to the Admiralty Point Lighthouse. Or, keep walking the beach 0.5 mile to the long and bluffless beach at Camp Casey. At the start of this beach one can walk up to the grass and head right just above the beach to find a

Admiralty Point Lighthouse

path leading back up to the lighthouse for a 1.2-mile loop. Or just keep following the beach northward as far as time and tides allow. Ebey's Landing is approximately 2.0 miles beyond the Camp Casey Beach (or 3.0 miles from the gun batteries).

WHIDBEY ISLAND—
75. Keystone Spit

Distance: 0.5 to 2.6 miles round trip
Time: 1 to 2 hours
Elevation gain: none
NOTE: CHECK THE TIDE TABLES BEFORE HEADING OUT...

Just east of the Keystone Ferry, a 1.7-mile-long spit encloses Crockett Lake, formerly a shallow lobe of Admiralty Bay that is now Whidbey Island's largest lake. Oddly enough, this low-lying spit was platted in 1890 as "New Chicago," a conceptual city that was supposed to boom with the development of an island railroad that was never built. Neither did Whidbey's Chicago materialize, though a few homes were constructed in the 1970s—much to the despair of nature- loving islanders who preferred the lake and beach just the way they were. The land was finally acquired in the 1980s for public enjoyment and preservation. Although SR 20 divides the beach from the lake, marine and freshwater habitats provide good birding much of the year.

Follow SR 20 or SR 525 and the signs to the Keystone-Port Townsend Ferry and look for the Fort Casey State Park boat launch immediately east of the terminal and opposite the west end of Crockett Lake. The rest of Fort Casey State Park lies to the west of the terminal (see Hike 74). One could park at the boat launch and walk a short section of beach here, but for the full trek, head east on SR 20 less than a half-mile to a signed park road leading to a T; turn right to find a small interpretive display and a good spot to begin the walk. The sand and gravel beach is quite walkable at a five-foot tide, but if the water is much higher a rough path behind a driftwood- laden berm is reasonably negotiable just about any time. Accessible beach ends at a primitive county park site (Driftwood Park) after 1.3 miles. On a good day, Port Townsend and the Olympic Mountains are prominent across the inlet. An interpretive display identifies the peaks.

Whidbey Island—
76. Wilbert Trail
Distance: 0.7 to 3.0 mile loops
Time: 1 to 2 hours
Elevation gain: minimal to 300 feet

Visit South Whidbey State Park in the off-season and you may well have the entire place to yourself. With more than 50 campsites nicely spaced under the canopy of an old-growth forest, South Whidbey makes an excellent retreat from a scurried life in the city. But like so many other pretty places, the park can fill up quickly on any summer weekend. But regardless of the season or whether staying for an hour or several days, a walk in the old growth by way of the Wilbert Trail is mandatory (*see back cover photo, upper left*).

Find South Whidbey State Park on the island's west shore midway between Greenbank and Freeland. Follow SR 525 to either community then head west on Smugglers Cove Road from Greenbank at about milepost 26, or on Bush Point Road from Freeland at milepost 19, and follow the signs a few miles to the park entrance. From the main parking area, several options are feasible. The Wilbert Trail alone is just under a mile long, but makes a 1.4-mile loop getting to and from the end points. One can add about 0.6-mile to the hike by including the Forest Discovery Loop, and another mile by adding the Ridge Loop, for a total hike of 3 miles. The longer loop is described below, but vary it as you like. (Note that the distances shown on the park trail map can be confusing.)

From the parking area find the Forest Discovery Trail heading left from the amphitheater (near the Beach Trail). The trail runs the edge of the bluff with good views of Admiralty Inlet and the Olympic Mountains, then swings around a ravine to a junction. Left heads 50 yards to the park entrance, but go right and right again for the rest of this short loop, then head for the entrance. The Wilbert and Ridge Loop Trails begin on the other side of Smugglers Cove Road. Wilbert is the easier, prettier loop and includes interpretive sites highlighted in a park brochure (box nearby). There are some very large Douglas fir trees along with a few red cedar, hemlock, and Sitka spruce scattered about in this exceptional forest. For the longer hike, take the Ridge Loop, built in the late 1990s by volunteers with the Central Whidbey Trails Council, then return via Wilbert.

The Ridge Loop ambles upward to an old logging area, rapidly being reclaimed by red alder and salmonberry. Fortunately, the land here was acquired by the park before the old forests on either side were destroyed. The trail follows the former logging road, passes a service road, then descends to meet the Wilbert Trail at a giant fir tree, 0.5 mile (via the latter) from the park entrance. Logic would suggest heading left and back to the start, but the best part of the Wilbert Trail is to the right. Walk this past more big trees, including a five-foot Douglas fir that, oddly, was cut and left to rot. About 0.4 mile from the last junction a sign points to a large ancient cedar tree on the left. At this point, either retrace your steps (recommended) and follow the Wilbert Trail back to the park entrance, or descend a short distance to Smugglers Cove Road and a path leading into the campground. Amble left here to find the main parking area.

WHIDBEY ISLAND—
77. Admiralty Inlet Beach

Distance: 0.6 to 2.5 miles round trip

Time: 1 to 3 hours

Elevation gain: 300 feet

NOTE: CHECK THE TIDE TABLES BEFORE HEADING OUT...

If you just need a little fresh air and a short workout, the beach at South Whidbey State Park is a worthy choice. The park is perched on a lovely forested bluff about 300 feet above the sea, which is where the workout comes in. (See Hike 76 for directions to the park, and for other short hikes in the old-growth forest.) From the big parking lot, the signed beach trail would be hard to miss.

The wide smooth path descends moderately a short distance to a junction. Head left for the beach, or hard right to the campground. Or, for an extra bit of exploring, take a soft right, cross a footbridge, and find the Hobbit Trail just ahead on the left, next to a campsite. This trail drops more steeply about 0.1 mile to an overlook with a partial view northward to the beach below. Back at the last junction, continue down an easy 0.25 mile to the beach. Gaze at the Olympics. Wander aimlessly. Watch barges and freighters churning the waters of Admiralty Inlet. Check out the tideland ecosystem.

The park's mile-long beach is inviting in both directions, though you will eventually run into civilization and the requisite "private beach" signs if you go too far. Walk the beach about 0.4 mile south to a giant green boulder, perhaps carried here and dumped by a melting glacier thousands of years ago. Bush Point is visible farther south. The bluffs are a reminder of the huge glaciers that more than once buried the Puget lowland landscape under thousands of feet of ice, then melted and retreated, leaving behind hundreds of feet of sediments throughout the region. Don't forget to save some energy for the climb back up the ancient bluff.

WHIDBEY ISLAND—
78. Double Bluff
Distance: 0.5 to 4 miles round trip

Time: 1 to 3 hours

Elevation gain: none

NOTE: CHECK THE TIDE TABLES BEFORE HEADING OUT...

One of several classic beach walks on Whidbey Island, Double Bluff is a must for any self- respecting beach-goer, with two miles of public tidelands, much sandy beach, and huge flats during low tides. The bluffs front on Useless Bay, and the shallow water here can warm to swimmable temperatures in sunny summer weather. As nice as the beach is with its expansive views across Admiralty Inlet, it is the abrupt 400-foot-high bluffs that make this place such a draw. The bluffs are actively eroding, with some areas losing as much as a foot each year. Composed of sediment deposits from at least 300,000 years of advancing and retreating glaciers, the bluffs nicely illustrate the story of this relatively recent geological past—and present.

To reach the Double Bluff Beach Access (an Island County Park), follow SR 525 to Double Bluff Road about eight miles northwest of the Clinton ferry dock; turn south and find the parking area in just under two miles. There is only room for about 20 cars so you may want to avoid the area on those sunny summer weekends, or at least arrive early. Biking is also an option; it's a 10-mile ride each way from the ferry to the beach. An interpretive sign near the restrooms explains some basic bluffery, like the relationship of eroding bluffs and accreting beaches in the Puget Sound region. It is also believed that Double Bluffs lie along a major active fault that could generate powerful earthquakes greater than magnitude 6.0. With small and large chunks of earth regularly falling from above, it's wise to give the base some breathing room.

If you time your walk with lower tides, say less than two or three feet (check the tide tables), there is much to explore and plenty of firm wet sand to walk on, though the beach becomes a bit rockier as you go. Pass beneath the neck-craning bluffs as far as you like,

Beach at Double Bluff

while enjoying the open view across the water to the distant tops of buildings in downtown Seattle, resembling a bizarre cluster of totems on the horizon. After 0.5 mile or more, large slabs of ancient, compressed peat lie partly buried in the beach. At about 1.5 miles (an hour from the start), the bluff diminishes considerably then rounds a sharp point known as South Double Bluff; North Double Bluff is visible a half-mile away. Signs of civilization are apparent above the precipice, but the beach remains wild to the next point. Be sure you've reserved sufficient time for the walk back before dark, and before a higher high-tide floods most of the beach.

WHIDBEY ISLAND—
79. Indian Point
Distance: 0.5 to 4 miles round trip

Time: 1 to 3 hours

Elevation gain: none

NOTE: CHECK THE TIDE TABLES BEFORE HEADING OUT...

The high, eroding bluffs south of Indian Point have released a number of large slides in recent years, and debris still covers much of the upper beach area—in some places burying thousands of square yards of beach under thousands of tons of earthly sluff. The walk below these active cliffs offers a powerful lesson in coastal geology. Key concepts: glaciation, deposition, erosion, gravity. The process is virtually identical to what is under way at Double Bluff (see Hike 78) and elsewhere around Washington's inland sea. While the net result is beautiful and interesting to look at, the crumbling can be humbling.

The walk begins at Dave Mackie Memorial Park southwest of Clinton. From SR 525 (MP 12.3), turn south on Maxwelton Road and find the park on the right about 4.5 miles ahead. The bluff to the north is an attractive option, but head left (south) for Indian Point. Homes front the first half-mile of accretion beach before the bluff makes an abrupt appearance as you round the point. The high wall is an imposing sight. Bald eagles often perch in trees high above, and great blue herons frequent the shallow water, taking small fish with quick stabs of the beak. Mount Rainier rises above the mainland, and tall buildings of downtown Seattle spike the horizon to the right. The Olympics loom to the southwest, and Double Bluff is clearly visible to the northwest across Useless Bay.

One can turn back here for the shorter walk, or keep going 1.5 miles to Maple Point, now visible as a low point of land jutting toward Puget Sound. The evidence of landslides continues, and in one section a jumble of ancient peat is scattered across the beach. Higher tides and waves are gradually tidying things up, but prudence would suggest staying well back from the base. Just before Maple Point, the sandy beach disappears under a slippery flat of round rocks and

Indian Point beach

green algae which make the going more cumbersome. The point makes a good turnaround, though the bluff continues another half-mile before civilization is re-encountered at another stretch of beach homes.

As suggested above, plan your walk for a lower tide, and avoid the area entirely during stormy periods or higher tides. For a wider, more enjoyable beach to saunter, tidal elevations below five feet or so are recommended (check the tide tables, and see the note on beach access in What to Know Before You Go). In early spring watch for large flocks of Bonaparte gulls and Brant geese gathering and chattering near the tideline, plotting their annual return to the far north.

Yellow Island

San Juan County

With a reputation for lovely spring wildflowers, the Nature Conservancy's Yellow Island Preserve, northwest of Shaw Island, is a must for every island-naturalist. The walk, two easy loops, totals about 0.5 mile. From April to mid-May, these little fields of color are famously striking. An absence of browsing deer and livestock, and carefully controlled access, explain part of the reason more than 150 species of flowering plants thrive here, along with nearly as many birds and other wildlife species that feed and breed on and around Yellow Island's 10 acres. Seals sun on the rocks nearby and even give birth and nurse their young on Yellow's eastern spit. Orcas occasionally pass by. A caretaker/naturalist resides on site at an historic cabin. Guided natural history trips to Yellow Island and other beauty spots in the Wasp Islands are also available from Friday or Deer Harbors (or contact the Nature Conservancy in Seattle).

Yellow Island—
80. Wildflower Trail

Distance: 0.5 mile loop

Time: 1 hour

Elevation gain: minimal

The walk around Yellow Island is almost too short to list in a hiking book, but the experience is unique and worthy of mention. To protect this sensitive environment while accommodating public enjoyment, there are some rules to be aware of before you arrive. First, you can only visit the island between 10:00 am and 4:00 pm. Landings are generally restricted to the main southeast beach (it's okay to pull your kayak or dinghy up on the east spit fall through spring, but not between June 15 and August 15, in order to protect the seals). There is also no camping, fires, or pets allowed, nor can you collect anything (but photos). And don't plan on soaking up the rays on the beach once you have hiked the trail. You can't nap,

Yellow Island beach

snack, smoke, or pee on Yellow Island. In other words, you can mosey, but you can't linger. The rules are strict, but this is an ecological preserve, not a park. Despite hundreds of visitors coming to the island during peak flower season, human disturbance has been kept to a minimum, and that keeps the flowers blooming and birds singing year after year.

From the south beach, wander left and up the stone steps to begin the loop. A small wooden box contains brochures that guide you along the way. The caretaker's residence is to the left, a remarkable driftwood and stone structure built by Lewis and Tib Dodd in the late 1940s for $300 (they paid $8,000 for the island). This was their home until Lewis passed away in 1960. Tib moved on but visited the island frequently until the 1980s, shortly after the island was acquired by the Conservancy for preservation. Tib died in 1989 at the age of 94 knowing the island was protected; their ashes remain on the island they dearly loved.

The loop trail rounds the north end of the island and returns through trees to a junction near an interpretive sign. Head left before the sign for the second loop and a spur to the east spit. Thick patches of white fawn lilies and buttercup in late March are replaced

by chocolate lilies, scarlet paintbrush and shooting stars in April, followed by blue camas, chickweed, desert parsley, starflower, yarrow, stonecrop, gumweed, Hookers onion, and others as the season proceeds. In mid-June, the San Juan's rare prickly-pear cactus blooms, then quickly fades.

Hiking the San Juan Islands

Parks, Viewpoints, Water Access, & Campgrounds

Once you've hiked your socks off in the islands (perhaps literally), there are still plenty of great places to explore for their parks, views, water access, and campgrounds. More than 120 of these sites are listed here. Many are within a skip or two of the walks and hikes described in this guide.

Park listings include local, state, and federal recreation sites which may or may not include picnic areas, restrooms, car access, boat docks, launch, mooring buoys, or other facilities. Some are undeveloped and offer nothing more than a good view or a small beach to gawk at, though even these can be good for wildlife viewing or just a breath of fresh air. Almost any location in the islands could be called a viewpoint, so the purpose here is to highlight those areas that offer something unique or especially scenic.

Water access includes both freshwater lakes and marine sites that offer either foot access or boat access to a beach and/or water body. Trailerable and hand-launched boat access is noted, along with parking availability. But beware, many of these sites may be very small or crowded in fair weather, or may be inappropriate for larger craft. This is not a boaters guide, so be sure to consult other sources when planning your island boating adventures. Campgrounds include only those locations designed and maintained for overnight use. Expect to pay a fee and don't be surprised if sites fill up quickly on weekends or during good weather. As with all public facilities, leave no trace of your visit.

Allan Island
Immediately south of Burrows Island near Anacortes, Allan Island is entirely private and inaccessible, including tidelands.

Bare Island
A rock northwest of Orcas Island, within the National Wildlife Refuge and off limits.

Barnes Island
East of Orcas Island, Barnes is an entirely private island surrounded by public tidelands, most of which are rocky and inaccessible.

Battleship Island
A small National Wildlife Refuge island, northwest of San Juan Island, off limits.

Blakely Island
A large, mostly private island; extensive public tidelands, but no facilities. See Hike 1.

Blind Island
A 3-acre islet that was once a squatter's little estate, Blind Island is now a marine state park with four campsites, a composter outhouse, and a 360-degree view. Remnant cherry, apple, and hazelnut trees, a flowerbed, a diversity of native trees, and a splash of spring wild-

flowers remain on the island. A faint path loops around the meadowy summit, which offers a great view of Mount Baker and the Sisters Range beyond Harney Channel. At the mouth of Shaw Island's Blind Bay, Blind Island has only one tiny beach (on the west side) to land on at higher tides, and barely one or two more (on the south end) at lower tides. As part of the Cascadia Marine Trail system, the island is a popular stopover for kayakers.

BURROWS ISLAND

A mostly private island near Anacortes' Washington Park. The only public land is at the old light station above the southwest shore. Few beaches and a steep rocky coastline makes access difficult and unappealing.

CAMANO ISLAND

Livingston Bay—A small beach access and viewpoint on the north end of Camano Island with no facilities. The unsightly site is just off SR 532 on Fox Trot Way.

English Boom—An undeveloped 7-acre woodland and saltmarsh with strong potential for trails and nature observation; planned for future development by Island County. Watch for it (soon?) off the end of Moore Road, north of SR 532.

Utsalady Point Park—Find this small viewpoint park with picnic tables, outhouse, lawn area, a pretty garden, but a dastardly chainlink fence that spoils the view, follow North Camano Drive to Utsalady Point Road; turn north and head straight one block to the park.

Utsalady Point Boat Ramp—A small Island County boat ramp with very limited parking. Leave North Camano Drive at Utsalady Point Road and head right, then down the hill to find the launch area close by. Adjacent beaches are private.

Maple Grove Boat Ramp—From North Camano Drive, turn at Maple Grove Road (narrow, steep) and find this Island County boat ramp at the bottom of the hill in 0.5 mile. Adjacent beaches are private.

Cavalero Beach County Park—A small beach access with picnic tables and boat launch on central Camano's east shore. Head south on East Camano Drive, turn left on Cavalero Road, left again at the park sign.

Camano Island State Park—A large state park with extensive facilities, including trails, picnic tables, beaches, camping, boat launch, vistas, and old-growth forest. The original park was built by almost 900 volunteers in one day in 1949. See Hike 2 for directions.

Walter G. Hutchinson County Park—This small, minimally developed park on southern Camano Island offers a 0.3-mile of paths in pretty forest; no facilities. Park off East Camano Dr. just south of Dallman Road.

CANOE ISLAND

Tidelands around Canoe Island southeast of Shaw Island are all public, but generally rocky and difficult to access. The island's 45 wooded acres are private with no public facilities. The island is conspicuous from South Beach County Park, less than a half-mile away on Shaw Island, and from the beach leading to Flat Point on Lopez Island, 0.25 mile to the southeast (the shortest crossing for Shaw-bound paddlers).

CEMETERY ISLAND

A tiny undeveloped island park southeast of Stuart; no facilities, no camping.

CENTER ISLAND

A small, privately owned island west of Decatur with an undeveloped recreation site on the west shore. Public tidelands surround the island, rocky on the north, with walkable portions on the south side.

CLARK ISLAND

Clark Island Marine State Park—See Hike 5.

CLIFF ISLAND

A small private island off southwest Orcas Island with no public beach of interest.

COON ISLAND

A tiny private island southwest of Orcas, with public tidelands, but mostly rocky with pocket beaches only.

CRANE ISLAND

Nearly a mile across, Crane Island is somewhat comparable to nearby Jones Island, except that it is entirely private with only limited public tidelands on the north and west where only small pocket beaches are accessible. Southwest of Orcas Island.

CYPRESS ISLAND

Pelican Beach—The most popular boat access to Cypress Island (unprotected mooring buoys). Pleasant beach, boardwalk, barrier-free composter outhouse, seven campsites, interpretive facilities, and access to the island's extensive trail system. See Hikes 6 and 7.

Eagle Harbor—A more protected moorage on the northeast shore of Cypress Island, with a nice beach but no camping. Good access to the island's trails. See Hikes 7 and 8.

Cypress Head—A scenic headland on the east side of Cypress Island with ten campsites, two small beaches, partially protected boat moorage, and access to the island's trail system. See Hike 9.

DECATUR ISLAND

A mostly private island with a public dock, limited road system, and several walkable beaches. See also Hike 10.

DECEPTION ISLAND

A wild, undeveloped islet west of Deception Pass and part of the state park, but generally inaccessible due to steep rocky shores all around.

DOE ISLAND

Doe Island Marine State Park—A 6-acre island and marine state park southwest of Doe Bay, Orcas Island. Find a dock, seasonal float, a few excellent campsites, outhouse, and a short trail system (see Hike 11). Boaters access the island's dock from the east side due to shallow water to the west. Rowers and paddlers can land at minuscule rocky beaches on the south and southeast shores.

DOUBLE ISLAND

Near the entrance to Orcas Island's West Sound, Double Island(s) is/are privately owned, though its/their rocky tidelands are public. Little here of interest to hiker(s).

FIDALGO ISLAND

Cap Sante Park—A little gem of a park in Anacortes with trails, beach access, picnic area, and a popular overlook. From Commercial Avenue, head east on 4th Street and continue up the hill to a T intersection. Turn right to find the overlook in 0.5 mile. See also Hike 12.

Washington Park—A large City of Anacortes park occupying Fidalgo's Rosario Head, with several miles of rocky coastline, beaches, mature-foreste uplands, rocky meadows, trails, picnicking and play areas, boat launch with overnight parking, camping, vistas, and a 2.5-mile scenic drive (or bike). Find the park on Sunset Avenue less than a mile west of the San Juan Ferry Terminal. Most facilities are accessible from the parking areas near the entrance, or continue biking or driving the loop road past several overlooks, picnic spots, and trail crossings. The best views from the road are at 0.5 mile, 0.7 mile (Green Point), and 1.9 miles (Burrows Island). The bedrock beach along the north side is particularly enjoyable to explore at lower tides. See also Hike 13.

Tugboat Park—A City of Anacortes waterfront park with a basic lawn area, several benches, picnic tables, and a small sandy beach on Burrows Bay. One can also launch a kayak here with a short carry; park your vehicle on the road shoulder. From Sunset Avenue just west of the San Juan Ferry Terminal, turn south on Anaco Beach Road, then right on Doon Way to find the park down the hill on the left.

Cranberry Lake—A small lake surrounded by Anacortes Community Forest Lands. No facilities, other than trails and hand-launching for small boats. See Hike 14 for a loop around the lake.

Mount Erie Park—Another outstanding park maintained by the City of Anacortes, Mount Erie is within the Anacortes Community Forest Lands, and is both a well-known landmark and, at 1,270 feet, the highest point on Fidalgo Island. The wildland park is developed with trails and a steep winding road to a spectacular summit vista, but no other facilities. The mountain is also popular with rock climbers. See Hike 16 for directions.

Anacortes Community Forest Lands—In addition to Mount Erie, a number of lakes and extensive forests and wetlands are protected from development within more than 2,000 acres of Anacortes Community Forest Lands—a tremendous natural amenity for any community. Many miles of trails link a variety of destinations touched on only briefly in this guide (for more, watch for the new guide, *Hiking Skagit County*). For an introduction to the area, see Hikes 14, 15, and 16.

Heart Lake State Park—A small, minimally developed park near Mount Erie, with a boat launch, outhouse, trails, and a stand of old-growth Douglas fir at the south end. See Hike 15 for more.

Lake Erie—At the foot of Mount Erie, this placid, semi-developed lake can be reached at a fishing access and boat ramp off Rosario Road 0.3 mile west of the junction of Lake Campbell and Heart Lake Roads. An annual WDFW permit is required to use this site.

Lake Campbell—A large developed lake with an island (on an island) and plenty of noisy, fast boats towing happy water skiers on sunny summer weekends. No swimming allowed. The Fish and Wildlife boat access is off Campbell Lake Road 0.7 mile from SR 20 at milepost 46.1. An annual WDFW permit is required to use this site.

Sharpe Park—A small Skagit County park off Rosario Road, north of Rosario Beach. A quiet place for a picnic with the kids, plus a great trail to wetlands and an island overlook. See Hike 17.

Rosario Beach—Part of Deception Pass State Park, Rosario offers beach and trail access, a small dock, picnic areas, restrooms, and scenic views. See also Hike 18.

Pass Lake—A small, well known lake adjacent to SR 20 at the west entrance to Deception Pass State Park. There are no facilities other than a gravel parking area, short trails, and launching for hand-carried boats. Access is at the intersection of SR 20 and Rosario Road.

Flattop Island

East of Spieden Island, Flattop is within the National Wildlife Refuge and off limits.

Freeman Island

A cute little islet and undeveloped state park frequented by resort-goers from nearby Orcas Island (near West Beach). Shores are mostly rocky with little to offer in the way of beaches or moonlight strolls.

Frost Island

A privately owned, steep, rock island off the end of Lopez Island's Spencer Spit. Although the tidelands are public, the rugged shore precludes any real wandering. Determined paddlers can edge into the shore for a close look, but not much more.

Goose Island

Offshore of San Juan's Cattle Point and owned by The Nature Conservancy, Goose Island off limits to visitors like us.

Gossip Island

This tiny islet southeast of Stuart is an undeveloped marine state park; pretty to look at, but little to do if you land. No camping.

Guemes Island

Reached by the short ferry from Anacortes, Guemes offers several walkable beaches, quiet roads, and a small beach access at Young Park on the north end. See Hike 20.

Henry Island

A private island with an inaccessible lighthouse reserve and only limited tidelands, Henry offers no public facilities and very little in the way of beach rambling. The island is just off the northwest shore of San Juan Island and is generally of more interest to boaters (and residents) than trailsters.

Hope Island

A smallish, undeveloped island park east of Deception Pass State Park, of interest to hopeful kayakers. A path winds through forest, accessible from a gravel beach on the south side. Camping is not permitted.

James Island

James Island Marine State Park—Just east of Decatur Island, James Island State Marine Park is a popular boaters destination, with camping, trails, beach, forest, and first-class island archipelago scenery. The 113-acre island is also a stop on the Cascadia Marine Trail, and is known for its thriving colony of pesky raccoons. Again, currents and rips are frequent near James. Hand-launchers can put in at either Spencer Spit or the Hunter Bay county dock on Lopez Island. For more information, see Hike 21.

Johns Island

Immediately east of Stuart Island across John's Pass is Johns Island, another private paradise surrounded by public tidelands. There are no public facilities. The more adventurous among us will find a few pleasant beaches broken up by rocky headlands. Access to the island requires a modest crossing of exposed water with copious rocks and shoals, and the possibility of strong currents and rips. Plan accordingly.

Jones Island

Jones Island Marine State Park—East of Decatur Island, Jones is an island park popular with boaters. The park includes scenic trails, beaches, camping, two docks with floats, and mooring buoys. See Hike 22.

Lopez Island

Odlin Park—A popular San Juan County park with trails, sandy beach, lawn areas, forested and beachfront campsites (plus bike and walk-in sites), restrooms, a boat ramp, and adjacent county dock and float. Odlin is just over a mile from the ferry landing and is a good place to launch a kayak (small fee for overnight parking). See also Hike 23.

Spencer Spit—A well-known Washington state park, and formerly an historic homestead, on the northeast shore of Lopez, with trails, beach areas, camping (including bike and walk-in sites), restrooms, and a launch area for car-top boats. The park is also on the Cascadia Marine Trail. See also Hike 24.

Hummel Lake Preserve—A preserve recently acquired by the San Juan County Land Bank to help protect Lopez Island's largest lake. Facilities include a loop trail, parking, bike rack, restroom, dock, and float. No camping, and no swimming or boating from the dock. A diversity of waterfowl and upland birds can be expected, depending on the season. The lake is a placid scene, although traffic noise on Center Road is a disturbance at times. The top of Mount Baker is visible in the distance, above Cypress Island. From the ferry dock, head south 2 miles to a curve, turn left on Center Road. In about 2 more miles find the parking area on the left, 0.4 mile past Hummel Lake Road; separate bike access 100 yards before the turn. Trail is unpaved, but barrier-free. Fishing access to Hummel Lake is found at the southeast corner of the intersection of Center and Hummel Lake Roads.

Lopez Village—The urban heart of Lopez Island with plenty of good eateries (bring an appetite), 4 miles from the ferry dock. The west end of the village boasts a museum, a park with restrooms, public showers (summer only, bring coins), and parking. A public right-of-way and viewpoint exists nearby, but a steep bank makes it difficult to access the beach.

Weeks Wetland Preserve—Acquired by the San Juan County Land Bank, this wetland preserve next to Lopez Village borders the north end of Fisherman Bay. A bike rack, 0.1–mile trail, and interpretive signs provided; no dogs allowed. To find the trailhead, turn south on the paved road near the west end of the Village. The trail is close by on the left.

Fisherman Bay Beach—An inconspicuous beach access is located across the road and 50 yards south of the Weeks Wetland Trailhead (see above) at Lopez Village. The site offers a picnic table and potential kayak launch at the narrow mouth of Fisherman Bay. Adjacent beaches are private and parking is very limited (day use only). It is also a good place for paddlers to come ashore for groceries or goodies at the Village.

Otis Perkins Park/Fisherman Bay—An undeveloped San Juan County park with beach access and limited parking, but no other facilities. See Hike 25 for directions.

Shark Reef Sanctuary—A Washington DNR recreation site, minimally developed with a trail, outhouse, and very limited parking. See Hike 26 for directions.

Hunter Bay Dock—A San Juan County dock near the point between Hunter and Mud Bays on South Lopez Island. The site receives frequent use, has a dock, float, boat ramp, and modest parking area (72-hour maximum); a good launch for paddlers exploring south Lopez, Decatur, and James Islands. Follow Mud Bay Road to Islandale Road to find the dock 1.3 miles ahead.

Mud Bay/Shoal Bight Viewpoint—Lack of parking and other facilities makes this site perhaps of more interest to cyclists than non-cyclists. Follow Mud Bay Road to its end (becomes Sperry Road) where a narrow road continues across the tombolo to former Camp Nor'wester. The road and beach ahead are private, although locals have enjoyed using these Shoal Bight/Rosario Strait beaches for generations. Do not proceed past signs that say your presence is not welcome. Before the end of the paved road where it bends right, a narrow dirt track leads to the edge of Mud Bay for another perspective on the quiet side of Lopez. Tidelands to the left are public for about one mile. The tidelands become less walkable (mucky) toward the head of the bay.

Mackaye Harbor Boat Ramp—For a good spot to launch a small boat for southern Lopez explorations, try the San Juan County boat ramp and float at Mackaye Harbor. There is a large parking area but no other facilities (72-hour parking may be feasible). A short stretch of public beach near Johns Point and Barlow Bay to the southwest. From Mud Bay Road, turn right on Mackaye Harbor Road and right again at the boat ramp sign.

Agate Beach County Park—Continuing south on MacKaye Harbor Road (see above), reach this tiny day-use park above the beach about 1.7 miles from Mud Bay Road. Picnic tables, outhouse, and access to about 600 feet of public beach (gravel) are provided.

Blackie Brady Memorial Beach—This small beach access on Hughes Bay can be reached from Watmough Bay Road. Turn south off Mud Bay Road onto Aleck Bay Road, then continue straight at the next two intersections before bending right onto a gravel road leading to the small parking area. A long staircase heads down to the narrow beach between rock walls. Day use only.

Watmough Bay—Public lands near this scenic bay on southeastern Lopez Island were recently augmented with an acquisition by BLM and the Land Bank. A short beach is now available to the public at the end of a 0.2-mile trail. See Hike 27 for directions.

Matia Island

Matia Island State Marine Park—A remote northern island park and wilderness; part of the island is managed by Washington State Parks and the rest is designated wilderness within the San Juan Islands National Wildlife Refuge and is off limits. The park includes beaches, a dock, seasonal float, mooring buoys, limited camping, composter outhouse, old-growth forest, and a mile-long loop trail. See Hike 28.

McConnell Island & Northwest McConnell Rock

Southwest of Orcas Island's Deer Harbor, McConnell Island is entirely private. The rugged tidelands on its south half are public though mostly inaccessible. Northwest McConnell Rock, on the other hand, is an undeveloped marine state park. This tiny island with a handful of trees is connected to McConnell Island at lower tides by a gravel tombolo with short beaches on either side (beach south of the tombolo is private). The Rock is a good lunch stop for hungry kayakers barred from snacking at nearby Yellow Island (Hike 80).

Oak Island

Near the mouth of Orcas' West Sound, tiny Oak Island is publicly owned (BLM), but undeveloped, probably of more value to pinnipeds than bipeds.

Obstruction Island

A private island "obstructing" the pass between Blakely and Orcas Islands; no facilities or beaches for public access.

Orcas Island

Point Doughty DNR Recreation Site—An attractive site on the northwest shore of Orcas Island with boat access only (on the south side). Trails wind through interesting forest and along the rugged coast. Camping and picnicking is also available. Currents and tide rips need to be considered before you launch the kayak.

Eastsound Boat Dock—A public dock and float at Eastsound off Haven Road.

North Beach—A small beach access off the end of North Beach Road, north of Eastsound. The spot offers a nice view and is popular for launching kayaks, but the small parking area fills up quick. Adjacent tidelands, unfortunately, are private.

Killebrew Lake—A small lake on southern Orcas, of more interest to fishers and birders than hikers. East of Orcas Village on the north side of Killebrew Lake Road.

Rosario—A well known historic resort near Moran State Park, built for Mr. Moran himself, includes a boat harbor, landscaped grounds, and the Moran mansion. See Hike 30.

Moran State Park—The largest state park in the San Juan Islands, Moran sprawls across more than 5,000 acres, encompassing the high point of the San Juans, Mt. Constitution. Campgrounds, picnic areas, interpretive facilities, swimming, hand-powered boating areas (Cascade and Mountain Lakes), scenic drive to an historic viewing tower at the summit, and 30 miles of trails, mostly hiker only (some are open to mountain bikes from September 15 to May 15). A number of trails are described in this guide. See Hikes 30–37.

Cascade Lake—Hand-launched boating, swimming, picnicking, and sunbathing are popular activities at this famous lake next to the road leading through Moran State Park. Just head for the park, you can't miss it. See Hike 30.

Mountain Lake—A small campground is located on the west shore of Mountain Lake in Moran State Park. A loop trail leads around the lake, with links to Twin Lakes and Mount Constitution. Basic facilities are provided (no RV dumps or utilities). See Hikes 32 and 33.

Mount Constitution Summit—A popular destination for Orcas Island, the summit of Mt. Constitution—highest point in the San Juans—is reachable by several trails, or by car and a short walk from the parking area. A stone wall overlook and historic view tower provide commanding views of the islands to the north, east and south, as well as views of the mainland U. S. and Canada, including Bellingham, Mount Baker, the North Cascades, and the B.C. Coast Range. From the Orcas ferry landing, follow the signs to Moran State Park in 13 miles, and the summit in 19 miles. See also Hikes 33–36.

Obstruction Pass DNR Recreation Site—A walk-in only campground on Orcas Island near Obstruction Pass; a bit more than 0.5 mile each way. Outhouses, picnic tables, fire pits, and beach access provided. See Hike 38.

Doe Bay—A public viewpoint at an historic private resort with basic accommodations for light travelers, including camping, yurts and cabins, as well as paths, views, eats, guided kayak trips, and outdoor hot tubs.

Patos Island

Patos Island Marine State Park—A remote northern park with camping (limited), outhouse, beaches, trails, lighthouse, dock, seasonal float, and mooring buoys. See Hike 39.

Posey Island

Only an acre in size, pretty Posey Island is a minimally developed state marine park with a single campsite and a good view—a great fair-weather destination for a light day of paddling, with relatively easy access from Roche Harbor. Launch your own craft, rent a sit-on-top kayak, or pay a guide to show you the way. The north side of the island looks out on Spieden Channel, its merging with Haro Strait, and Canada beyond. If you plan to camp, have a back-up plan in mind in case it's taken. Better yet, make it a day trip. Note that Roche Harbor can be a veritable zoo at times during the summer boating season.

PUFFIN ISLAND

A small National Wildlife Refuge island just offshore of Matia Island that is off limits.

RAM ISLAND

Another tiny island of interest to paddlers, Ram Island is 0.2 mile northwest of Lopez Island's Sperry Peninsula (just south of Decatur). Although the island is private, public access has been allowed (no fires or camping). A pocket beach on the southeast side affords a rocky landing, and a short path leads toward the south point and along the northeast side; the rest is brushy--don't trample. Nearby Rim and Rum Islands are within the San Juan Islands National Wildlife Refuge and are off limits to humanoids.

SAN JUAN ISLAND

Friday Harbor—The urban heart of the San Juans with a range of facilities and services for travelers. A good place to wander, with great shops, eateries, lodging, walkways, benches, viewpoints, a boat harbor, Whale Museum, Pig War Museum, and, the ferry terminal.

Roche Harbor—Another old resort that was once the site of lime kilns, quarries, and barrel-making industries that dominated much of the island's early history. Find a big boat harbor, the impressive Hotel de Haro and its fabulous garden, a market, kayak guides and rentals, a walking trail to overlook the old quarries (watch for the sign on the descent to the harbor), and another path leading past the airstrip to an old cemetery and odd mausoleum containing the ashes of the man who built the place (just follow the signs).

English Camp—The northerly unit of the San Juan Island National Historic Park, on the site of the British encampment during the so-called Pig War. Limited facilities, with access to Bell Point and Mount Young. See Hikes 40 and 41.

American Camp—The southerly unit of the San Juan Island National Historic Park, on the site of the American encampment during the Pig War. Limited facilities, but great views and extensive hiking opportunities. See Hikes 44–48.

Cattle Point—Before the famed San Juan pig was shot in 1859, Cattle Point was used by the British Hudson's Bay Company to load and off-load livestock. At the southerly tip of San Juan Island, the site is now better known for wide open views and a small historic lighthouse that aids navigation in Juan de Fuca Strait, Haro Strait, and San Juan Channel. A viewpoint and parking area offer a chance to see traveling orcas and roiling tide rips in San Juan Channel. An inconspicuous path nearby leads to the lighthouse. See Hike 45.

Lime Kiln Point State Park—A popular park and overlook on the site of an historic lime kiln operation, perfectly for viewing whales up close. Strong tidal currents, deep water, and a rich marine ecosystem make this an important feeding ground for orcas, with mid-May through September generally being the best time to see one--or twenty. A new barrier-free path leads to an overlook at the water's edge, though a poorly designed rock wall creates a visual barrier for some. Volunteers often assist with questions and information. Bring a good book and wait. Can be a little crowded on weekends. See Hike 42.

Deadman Bay—Adjacent to Lime Kiln Point State Park, with a path, restroom, and scenic beach. See Hike 42.

San Juan County Park (Small Pox Bay)—A small county park with a no-frills campground, a picnic area, and hand-launch boat access. Campsites are in very high demand in summer. Pretty coastline and good potential for orca viewing in the summer months.

Eagle Cove—A lovely little beach reached by a short walk (less than 0.1 mile) with a bit of rocky shore to explore. From Cattle Point Road, turn right on Eagle Cove Road just before entering the national historical park at American Camp. Find the signed parking area about 0.5 mile ahead on the left.

Ruben Tarte Beach—On the island's quiet northeast shore, this county-owned beach access (day-use only) is small but attractive for a picnic, a read, or perhaps to launch a kayak. From Roche Harbor Road, turn north on Rouleau Road, right on Limestone Point Road, and right again on San Juan Drive. The park is just ahead on the left. Note that there is no parking, except one handicap space, and only a small turnaround at the beach. Park above and walk down the short and steep, paved road.

Sportsmans Lake—A modest-sized lake northwest of Friday Harbor, Sportsmans Lake can be a busy place late spring and summer weekends. A steep, rough boat ramp is available, but very little parking. Find a big rock for contemplating career moves at water's edge left of the ramp. Some of the adjacent land has been acquired and set aside as the Sportsmans Lake Preserve by the San Juan Preservation Trust. The conspicuous lake is about four miles from Friday Harbor on the left side of Roche Harbor Road. No camping.

Egg Lake—Connected to Sportsmans Lake by a broad cattail marsh, Egg Lake feels less humanized than the former. A good place to fish, think, and paddle. A small dock and float are available next to a turn-out on Egg Lake Road, 0.6 mile south of its junction with Roche Harbor Road. No other facilities. Thanks are due Washington Department of Fish and Wildlife, San Juan Island Park and Recreation District, and the Lions Club.

SATELLITE ISLAND

Named for a British ship involved in the 1860s boundary dispute, Satellite Island protects Stuart Island's Prevost Harbor from whatever might blow in from Boundary Pass, and adds considerably to the harbor's scenery (Prevost was the ship's commander). Though its tidelands are public and there is some pleasant beach to explore, Satellite is privately owned (by the YMCA) and not developed for access by the general public. Beware of shallow water and rocks in the little pass east of the island. For more, see Stuart Island.

SENTINEL ISLAND

Acquired by The Nature Conservancy with Yellow Island in1980, Sentinel Island, near Spieden, is off limits to people.

SHAW ISLAND

South Beach County Park—A basic park and campground with about a dozen sites, boat ramp, picnic tables, outhouses, and a broad sandy beach—one of the few in the San Juans where the water warms enough to swim in on a sunny summer day. See also Hike 49.

Point George Biological Reserve (UW)—An ideal stop for naturalists, birders, and cyclists, the University of Washington reserve at Point George is generally open to visitors, though there are no facilities other than a trail register. Remember, this is a biological reserve, not a park. Bring the binoculars and enjoy it for its natural beauty, but disturb nothing. Parking is extremely limited, so it's best to visit by bicycle. From the ferry dock follow Blind Bay Road to Hoffman Cove Road, turn left, and continue to the road end above the cove; the gate is on the left. See also Hike 50.

Neck Point—A rare public beach access on Shaw Island at the far west end at Neck Point; no parking, though the site can be easily accessed by bike (or kayak) and affords a nice view north to Yellow Island and south into San Juan Channel. Public tidelands extend around the point, but rocky shores tend to limit access to areas closer to the road. The north side is attractive. A backwater area on the south side is choked with driftwood and better left to wildlife. From the ferry dock, Blind Bay Road eventually becomes Neck Point Road; follow it to the obvious, narrow neck of land near its end. The uplands are private.

SHEEP ISLAND

Another tiny neighbor of Orcas Island (within West Sound), Sheep is privately owned. Tidelands are public but unappealing.

SINCLAIR ISLAND

This Skagit County island is mostly private with some walkable beach on the south and west, and a wildlife preserve toward the north end (see Hike 51). A county dock and small float exist on the east shore, and a limited public road system (unpaved) accesses other parts of the island. There are no other public facilities, although Western Washington University students maintain a small beach house on the southwest shore. Enjoy a lazy stroll on the beach and island roads.

SKAGIT ISLAND

A tiny, pretty island east of Deception Pass State Park with no facilities and no camping allowed. A short path can be reached from small beaches on the east side.

SKIPJACK ISLAND

Another National Wildlife Refuge island north of Waldron, Skipjack is off limits to people.

SKULL ISLAND

A tiny, undeveloped marine state park at the head of Orcas Island's West Sound. Very limited access, no camping or fires allowed.

SPIEDEN ISLAND

Privately owned Spieden Island became famous (infamous?) during its short-lived status as Safari Island in the late 1960s when exotic African game animals were brought here for sport hunting—an idea that did not go over well with the public. The plan was quickly abandoned, but supposedly a few oddball deer from afar still live and breed on the island. A mile north of San Juan Island, Spieden is easily recognized at a distance by its extensive and uniformly unforested southern slope. About two miles of public shore exist along the northwestern part of the nearly 500-acre island, but access is difficult. There are no public facilities. Tiny Sentinel Island, just off the southwest shore, is owned by the Nature Conservancy and is off limits. The Cactus Islands and Flattop Island to the north and northeast are within the San Juan Islands National Wildlife Refuge and are also off limits.

STRAWBERRY ISLAND

Just off the southwest shore of Cypress Island, little Strawberry Island is a mostly wooded, minimally developed marine state park popular with kayakers; relatively easy access from Anacortes. Strong currents in Guemes and Bellingham Channels require careful planning. The island was named for Strawberry Bay, itself named by Vancouver for the wild fruit. A short path leads to campsites and explores part of the islet's steep, rocky shore. To visit this stop on the Cascadia Marine Trail, head for the small beach at the south end.

Stuart Island

Stuart Island Marine State Park—A remote island with a marine park popular with boaters; picnicking, camping, docks, floats, mooring buoys, restrooms, beaches, and trails sandwiched between two harbors. See Hike 52 for more.

Turn Point Lighthouse V—A lovely spot on Haro Strait. See Hike 53.

Sucia Island

Sucia Island Marine State Park—A spectacular island of multiple narrow coves and peninsulas, sculpted sandstone shores, and walkable beaches. Amenities include docks, floats, mooring buoys, camping, picnicking, interpretive facilities, and an extensive trail system. Its unique beauty discovered long ago, Sucia can be a crazy place on sunny summer weekends. Dogs must be on leashes. To conspire a visit, see Hikes 54–57.

Turn Island

Turn Island Marine State Park—A scenic 35-acre island only a mile and a half southeast of Friday Harbor, Turn Island is both a National Wildlife Refuge island (designated wilderness) and a marine state park. It is one of only two islands in the refuge that are accessible to the public (Matia is the other). The park includes picnic facilities, campsites, composter outhouses, a looped trail system, and several nice beaches. There is no dock, but a few mooring buoys can be found off the northwest shore. See also Hike 58.

Victim Island

Another tiny, undeveloped state park islet within Orcas Island's West Sound. Shores are rocky with little opportunity to explore.

Waldron Island

Waldron is one of the larger islands in the San Juans with next to nothing in the way of public facilities or walkable tidelands. The comparatively recluse island community has a reputation for being somewhat reluctant to welcome outsiders. Point Disney is a recent reserve success on the south end, though access is limited. Only a scrap of accessible public beach exists at the San Juan County dock in Cowlitz Bay. Waldron has a small amount of technically walkable, but difficult to access, public beach on the north end, including a half-mile chunk beginning just south of Point Hammond and heading south, and a similar stretch heading east from Fishery Point. Another half-mile rounds Sandy Point to the west.

Whidbey Island

Deception Pass State Park—The most heavily visited state park in Washington, Deception Pass has every virtue of a national park. More than 4,100 acres of paradise, including almost 15 miles of marine coast and 6.4 miles of freshwater shoreline encompass old-growth forests, extensive beaches, a sizeable lake (Cranberry), sand dunes, and some of Washington's most rugged coastline, as well as world-famous bridges spanning the namesake passage. Vertigo bridge-walking is a popular attraction; the recent addition of stairs and pedestrian underpasses at each end of the main bridge allows walkers to traverse both walkways without having to dodge traffic. Captain Vancouver was deceived, thinking this was a bay during an initial survey in 1792, thus the name when Joseph Whidbey determined otherwise. Facilities include over 200 campsites, picnicking, boat ramps, moorage, amphitheater, shelters, interpretive signs, some unsightly pop machines (their brightly lit fronts spoil the darkness), and nearly 30 miles of trails (see Hikes 18, 19, and 59–62). The main park entrance is off SR 20 at Cornet Bay Road, about a mile south of the bridge.

Ala Spit—A recent acquisition with no facilities other than a small parking area, and access to about a mile of scenic beach. See Hike 63.

Dugualla Bay Dike—Road turn-outs at the north and south ends of the dike supporting Dike Road provide a view of Dugualla Bay to the east, and a cut-off portion of the bay, called Dugualla Pond, to the west. Public tidelands extend a short distance along the east beach. Find Dike Road about a mile east of SR 20 via Frostad Road.

Whidbey Highlands & Dugualla Bay—A former DNR property purchased by Washington State Parks provides limited access to public tidelands on Dugualla Bay. There are no facilities. Find the site off Sleeper Road, 2.5 miles east of SR 20. The park is undeveloped and gated at the west end. To reach the beach walk, follow the old road 0.1 mile to a fork and stay right for 0.3 mile, then go left for 0.3 mile more to where the old road narrows to a path. Descend to a stately six-foot diameter Douglas fir, then more steeply to the beach, about 1.0 mile from the start. The last 100 yards may be somewhat overgrown. Overhanging trees can make the gravel beach difficult to negotiate at higher tides. Mark the trail so you can find it on the return. Goat Island lies across Skagit Bay with Mount Baker beyond.

Morans Beach—A small beach access at a road end south of Deception Pass State Park, adjoins private tidelands. From SR 20, take Banta to Moran Road, left on Powell Road.

Joseph Whidbey State Park—A minimally developed, 112-acre state park west of Oak Harbor (close to the Navy base), with picnic, lawns, paths, extensive beach and wetlands, restrooms, and a wide open view of the Strait of Juan de Fuca. See also Hikes 76 and 77.

West Beach Vista—Just south of Joseph Whidbey State Park, beyond a string of waterfront homes, is a small turnout with a view of what erosion can do to misplaced shoreline development. This site is a classic example of why concrete bulkheads are generally such a bad idea along marine shores. Mainly, they simply don't hold up to the nonstop whims of nature, and secondly, the whole mess is likely to turn into unsightly rubble where there was once a pretty beach. (One can only wonder about the homes to the north and south.)

City Beach Park (Oak Harbor)—A city park that ought to win an award for variety. Find ballfields, play and picnic areas, a wading pool, waterfront paths (some lighted), a campground, boat launch, a Dutch windmill, and an A-6E fighter jet. From the main traffic light where SR 20 bends to the west, head east on Pioneer Way about two blocks and turn right on City Beach Street. Plenty of beach to walk (see Hike 65).

Flintstone Park—A simple waterfront park just to the east of City Beach Park in Oak Harbor, but with only a hint of Bedrock City apparent. Find lawn and play areas, a few picnic tables, a beach, and a small boat dock.

Oak Harbor Marina—The main boat harbor, with a boat ramp, dock, walkways, benches, picnic tables, lawn and play areas, small beach, volleyball, and horseshoes; south of Pioneer Way at Catalina Drive.

Smith Park—An Oak Harbor city park in a modest grove of garry oak trees, includes lawns, play areas, picnic tables, walkways, and a gazebo. At 9th Avenue and Jensen Street.

Hastie Lake Beach Access—Island County beach access and small boat launch ramp, located at West Beach, at the west end of Hastie Lake Road southwest of Oak Harbor. Boaters should be alert for waves and wake that can complicate launching. See also Hike 66.

Monroe Landing—An Island County beach access and view across Penn Cove to Coupeville. See also Hike 65.

Libbey Beach Park—A small Island County park with a few tables, lawn area, restrooms, and access to West Beach (beach area closed for repairs in spring 2001.) See also Hike 67.

Fort Ebey State Park—An excellent state park on 645 acres near the Keystone-Port Townsend ferry terminal, with historic WWII gun batteries constructed in 1942, picnicking, 50 campsites (very nice), restrooms, interpretive signs, access to miles of public beach, and an extensive upland trail system of nearly 30 miles. The fort was donated by the Army to the state in 1968 and opened as a park in 1981. See Hikes 67–70 for more.

Ebey's Landing National Historical Reserve—An impressive historic reserve encompassing 17,400 acres--a broad swath of north-central Whidbey Island from Fort Ebey to Fort Casey and surrounding Penn Cove and the City of Coupeville. A visit to the museum in Coupeville is a worthwhile introduction to an area whose rich history was central to the development of northwest Washington. Pick up a brochure for a driving or biking tour to learn and see more, and to marvel at the great victory of the citizens who fought hard to protect the area from greedy developers. Refer to Hikes 65–74 for more.

Ebey's Landing—A self-guided scenic drive through the National Historic Reserve descends Hill Road to Ebey's Landing at the bottom of the hill next to the beach. A parking area nearby offers beach access and serves as a trailhead for hikes northward along the bluff. Find interpretive signs, restrooms, and viewing benches here as well. Just up the hill, south of the road, an historic home built by the original Ebey pioneers still stands.

Ebey's Prairie Overlook—High on a hill, next to Sunnyside Cemetery, enjoy a fine view of the namesake prairie that all this national historic fuss is about. Had there been no fuss, it all might have been tract homes by now. Thankfully, it isn't. See Hike 71 for more.

Prairie Wayside—A turn-out along the historic Ebey's Landing biking/driving tour, accessed from Engle Road just north of Hill Road. No facilities other than interpretive signs and a short path through wild rose bushes that offers an excellent view of the prairie.

Historic Coupeville—Downtown Coupeville offers much to explore on foot, a great museum (open every day May to September, Fri-Mon from October to April), plus a public wharf where the bones of a grey whale are nicely displayed, and a garden path leading to the town park. Find a map for the walking tour at the kiosk near the corner of Front and Alexander, or pick up a brochure at the museum across the street. See also Hike 73.

Coupeville Town Park—More than your basic town park, including picnic and play areas, a covered pavilion, community kitchen, tennis court, an 8-foot-diameter log round, and a short trail to the beach. The log round still shows the marks of an axe. It was moved here from Perego's Lagoon in the 1930s.

Thomas Coupe Park—While exploring Coupeville, one could also walk east along the waterfront a few blocks on a gravel path to Captain Thomas Coupe (as in Coupeville) Park, but there is only a restroom, small beach, and boat ramp here. A modest-sized parking area makes this a good spot to launch a boat on Penn Cove.

Rhododendron Recreation Area—This attractive but inconspicuous DNR site is tucked away in the island's interior forest about two miles southeast of Coupeville. Six campsites, picnic area, and outhouses are the principal amenities, though the area is downright lovely when the wild rhododendrons are blooming mid-May to mid-June. An unsigned road leads south off SR 20 0.3 mile east of Jacobs Road (watch for the small-blue camping signs) and reaches the site in 0.5 mile. A sign next to the road indicates a loop trail through the camping area but it is indistinguishable on the ground. A few boot trails wander the woods but offer little in the way of a hike. The area clearly warrants a maintained loop trail, perhaps linked to Island County's Rhododendron Park and a wildlife area nearby. For now, the best place to stroll (or bike) is along the scenic, single-lane paved road that continues 0.8 mile south to Patmore Road. Worth a visit, especially in rhodie season.

Rhododendron Park—A ho-hum park dominated by ballfields, oddly lacking in significant walking paths despite great potential for a stroll in pleasant forest and a sea of blooming rhododendrons during May and June. The 32-acre park is about a half-mile off SR 20 on Patmore Road, east of Coupeville. Trail links to a neighboring wildlife area and DNR's Rhododendron Recreation Area would add some appeal (see above).

Fort Casey State Park—Adjacent to the Keystone ferry terminal, Fort Casey is a popular and nicely developed state park rooted in history. It is one of several military defense installations constructed in the area during the first half of the twentieth century, but fortunately never called on to defend Old Glory. Gun batteries, bunkers, and related windowless structures can be explored by the public (a flashlight helps), along with surrounding forest, bluffs, and beaches. The 467-acre park includes 35 beachfront campsites (small sites in a compact area), picnicking, viewpoints, trails, interpretive facilities, and even an exhibit on composting next to the picturesque Admiralty Point Lighthouse, which now serves as a small interpretive center. Open year round, the park extends across the ferry dock to a day-use site (aka Keystone State Park), where you'll find restrooms with coin-op showers, a boat launch, more picnic facilities, a beach, and for diver-types, an underwater park just offshore. A good place to watch the ferries ferry, as giant freighters ply Admiralty Inlet close to shore. See also Hikes 74 and 75.

Keystone State Park—See Fort Casey State Park.

Driftwood Park—A small beach access area, courtesy of the Lions Club, at the east end of Keystone Spit. The gravel lot is just off SR 20, 1.8 miles east of the Keystone-Port Townsend ferry terminal. See Hike 75 for a 1.3-mile beachwalk along the spit.

Lake Hancock Overlook—Along SR 20 at milepost 26.2, find a generally ignored overlook of one of the more significant coastal marsh ecosystems in the state. Not a true lake, Hancock is mostly enclosed by a natural spit and provides unique habitat for both marine and upland species of plants and animals. The area was also used by the Whidbey Naval Air Station as a practice bombing range in the 1940s through 1960s. Mostly the "bombs" were inert sandbags, and a good part of the mess made has been cleaned up and restored over the years, so that the environment today is relatively pristine. The area remains closed to the public, but is still worth a quick stop and a look.

South Whidbey State Park—A fine state park with 54 excellent campsites in old-growth forest on a bluff overlooking Admiralty Inlet. The 347-acre park includes picnic areas, shelters, fire circles, amphitheater, restrooms, beach access, and forest trails. See Hikes 76 and 77 for more. Park facilities may be unavailable in winter, although the trails are open.

Lagoon Point—A small parking area provides access to about 400 feet of public tidelands and could be used to launch a kayak. From Smugglers Cove Road north of South Whidbey State Park turn west on Mountain View Road to find the site a half-mile below.

Freeland Park—A nice little park at the head of Holmes Harbor on south Whidbey Island, with a boat ramp, picnic and play areas, and a small beach to explore. Several roads lead to the park from nearby SR 20 at Freeland.

Mutiny Bay Boat Ramp—This small boat launch and parking area (1 block from the ramp) can be accessed from Robinson Road just south of the intersection of Mutiny Bay Road and Fish Road. Adjacent tidelands are private.

Double Bluff—An excellent viewpoint and beach walk begins at this Island County park on south Whidbey Island; see Hike 78 for directions.

Goss Lake—A small semi-developed lake west of Langley with a simple boat ramp. From Goss Lake Road, turn south on Pintail Road, then left on Lakeside.

Goss Lake area DNR lands—A maze of mountain biking and equestrian trails have been improved on nearly 600 acres of DNR land east of Lone Lake Road and north of Keller Road (a mile east of Goss Lake). The area could have growing appeal to hikers, depending on how it's managed.

Lone Lake—An attractive small lake west of Langley, of interest to boaters and fishers. Large lawn area and picnic tables, plus the boat ramp at this Island County park off Lone Lake Road. Head south from the bend where Lone Lake Road becomes Andreason Road.

South Whidbey Community Park—This large new regional park offers something for everyone: ballfields, horseshoes, picnicking and play areas, and about two miles of mostly multi-use trails. The park was still expanding in 2001 to include more fields and more trails. It's located between Langley and Maxwelton Roads, but access the park from Maxwelton, about 0.8 mile north of SR 525 (signed "parks and recreation entrance"). A 1.7-mile saunter in pretty forest is feasible from the trailhead at the end of the gravel road.

Langley Seawall Park—A small linear park easily accessed from First Avenue in downtown Langley. A grassy promenade links to boardwalk in front of condos, and a few stairs lead to 1,000 feet of public beach. Picnic tables and totem poles also.

Langley Park—Anyone for a walkable meditation maze? That plus some interesting art, flowers, and games at this little park on the corner of Second and Anthes Streets.

Phil Simon Memorial Park—This small, minimalist park on the Langley waterfront offers small boat access to Saratoga Passage (boat ramp), along with picnic tables, restrooms, and a short walkable pier next to the small boat harbor. Sorry, no overnight parking. Find the park at the end of Wharf Street below First Avenue.

Clinton Ferry Terminal—The ferry terminal at Clinton offers restrooms and a sheltered place for cyclists. In terms of a viewpoint, the ferry itself is obviously far better.

Dan Porter Park—A small town park at Clinton with ballfields, play area, restroom, and short paths. From SR 20, turn south on Deer Lake Road to find the park on the right.

Deer Lake—A small, mostly developed lake southeast of Clinton with a primitive launch. Follow Deer Lake Road about a mile from the ferry dock to Lake Shore Drive; turn right. The lake access is on the left.

Dave Mackie Memorial Park—Near the south tip of Whidbey, this simple waterfront park is mostly a ballfield, but there are restrooms, picnicking, a play area, and beach access as well. See Hike 79 for directions.

Possession Beach County Park—An attractive park near the southern tip of Whidbey Island, good for a picnic and a stroll on the beach, with potential to view the high bluffs at the point. At the time of publication, efforts were underway to expand the park to the south... stay tuned. From the road near the beach, a new path climbs a moderately up a forested ridge to a crest at 0.5 mile. From SR 525 (milepost 11.1), head south on Cultus Bay Road and follow the signs to the park.

Yellow Island

Yellow Island Preserve—A lovely island with limited access, famous for spring wildflowers. Acquired by The Nature Conservancy in 1980. Camping and picnicking are not allowed. Short loop trails provide a quick tour of the island's ecosystem. See Hike 80.

HIKING ORGANIZATIONS & AGENCIES

ALL EMERGENCIES—call 911

Ebey's Landing National Historical Reserve, www.nps.gov/ebla
Friends of the Anacortes Community Forest Lands, *619 Commercial Avenue, #32, Anacortes, WA 89221*
Guemes Island Ferry, *(360) 293-6356*
Island County Parks, *(360) 678-5111*, www.islandcounty.net
Island Transit, *(800) 240-8747, (360) 678-7771*, www.islandtransit.org
Marine Mammal Sightings Hotline *(800) 562-8832*
NOAA Weather, http://weather.noaa.gov/pd/waframes.html
San Juan County Land Bank, www.co.san-juan.wa.us/land_bank
San Juan County Park, *camp reservations, 7-90 days in advance: (360) 378-1842*
San Juan County Parks & Recreation, www.co.san-juan.wa.us/parks
San Juan Islands National Wildlife Refuge *(360) 457-8451*,
    www.pacific.fws.gov/visitor/washington.html
San Juan Preservation Trust, www.rockisland.com/~sjptrust
Skagit County Parks Department, *(360) 336-9414*,
    www.skagitcounty.net/offices/parks/index.htm
SKAT (Skagit Transit) *(360) 757-4433*, www.skat.org
The Nature Conservancy, *(206) 343-4344*, www.nature.org
U.S. Bureau of Land Management, www.or.blm.gov/spokane
U.S. Coast Guard www.uscg.mil
U.S. Fish & Wildlife Service, *general refuge information, (800) 344-9453*,
    http://refuges.fws.gov/wildlife.html
Washington Department of Fish & Wildlife, *(360) 902-2200*, www.gov/wdfw
Washington Department of Natural Resources, *(800) 527-3305*
    www.wa.gov/dnr
Washington State Ferries, *schedule & fare information, (800) 843-3779*,
    www.wsdot.wa.gov/ferries
Washington State Parks & Recreation Commission, *for campsite reservations
    at all state parks, call (800) 452-5687*; www.parks.wa.gov
    Camano Island State Park *(360) 387-3031*
    Deception Pass State Park *(360) 675-2417*
    Fort Casey State Park *(360) 678-4519*
    Fort Ebey State Park *(360) 678-4636*
    South Whidbey State Park *(360) 331-4559*
Washington Trails Association, www.wta.org
Washington Water Trails Association, www.wwta.org
Whale Museum (Friday Harbor), *(360) 378-4710*, www.whale-museum.org

FURTHER READING

Good references on boating in the region include **Exploring the San Juan and Gulf Islands: Cruising Paradise of the Pacific Northwest**, by Don Douglass & Réanne Hemingway-Douglass (Fine Edge Productions, 1998); the **Evergreen Pacific Cruising Guide: Washington Waters** (Evergreen Pacific Publishing, 1994); and **A Cruising Guide to Puget Sound: Olympia to Port Angeles Including the San Juan Islands**, by Migael Scherer (International Marine Publications, 1995). For boat launch information, try the website at <u>www.boat.iac.wa.gov</u>. Randel Washburne's **Kayaking Puget Sound, the San Juans, and Gulf Islands** (The Mountaineers Books, 1999) is a mandatory resource for paddlers. For cycling, try **Touring the Islands: Bicycling in the San Juan, Gulf, and Vancouver Islands**, by Peter Powers and Renee Travis (Terragraphics, 1991).

Several other guidebooks cover trails and beach walks in the islands, most notably Ted and Marge Mueller's **The San Juan Islands Afoot & Afloat** (The Mountaineers Books, 1998). E. M. Sterling's **Best Short Hikes in Washington's North Cascades & San Juan Islands** (The Mountaineers Books, 1994), Bob Mooers' **Winter Hikes in Puget Sound & the Olympic Foothills** (Sasquatch Books, 1998), and brief trail guides published by others. For Whidbey and Camano Island, check out Harvey Manning's **Walks & Hikes on the Beaches Around Puget Sound** (The Mountaineers Books, 1995). See also Jan Halliday's **San Juan & Gulf Islands Best Places: A Destination Guide** (Sasquatch Books, 1995). Most are available at libraries, book stores, boating and outdoor shops throughout the region.

No single volume sums up the history or prehistory of the San Juan Islands, though anecdotal histories area available for a number of islands individually. David Richardson's **Pig War Islands: The San Juans of Northwest Washington** (Orcas Publishing Company, 1990) is one of the better books around that address more than the oft-told story of the pig war. Other good sources include Harvey Manning's **Walking the Beach to Bellingham** (Madrona Publishers, 1986), and Julie K. Stein's **Exploring Coast Salish Prehistory** (University of Washington Press, 2000).

For natural history, try Evelyn Adams' **San Juan Islands Wildlife: A Handbook for Exploring Nature** (The Mountaineers Books/San Juan Preservation Trust, 1995); Scott Atkinson and Fred Sharpe's **Wild Plants of the San Juan Islands** (The Mountaineers Books/San Juan Preservation Trust, 1993); Pojar and MacKinnon's **Plants of the Pacific Northwest Coast** (Lone Pine Publishing, 1994); and Susan Vernon's **Wildlife Guide to the San Juans** (Archipelago Press), a handy map and guide to wildlife viewing in the islands.

INDEX

ABOUT THE AUTHOR

A resident of northwest Washington since 1967, Ken Wilcox is an avid explorer of the wildlands of the Pacific Northwest. When he isn't hiking trails and climbing mountains—habits that ought to last a lifetime—Ken works as a writer, consultant, and volunteer for a variety of environmental and recreation projects. He is also the author of **Hiking Snohomish County** (1998), the 3rd edition of **Hiking Whatcom County** (2000), and another book entitled **Chile's Native Forests: A Conservation Legacy** (1996). He lives in Bellingham.

Hiker's Log

Date	Trail	Miles	Notes